Judith Wills was editor of *Slimmer* magazine for over 10 years and now has a regular column in the magazine. She writes regularly for various magazines including *Prima* and *Woman*. She is the author of best-selling diet books including *A Flat Stomach in 15 Days, High Speed Slimming, Size 12 in 21 Days, Slim for Life* and *Fat Attack*. She has written three other cookery books – *Judith Wills 100 Favourite Slim and Healthy Recipes* (Piatkus), *Slim and Healthy Vegetarian* and *Slim and Healthy Mediterranean*. Her most recent title is *Take off 10 Years in 10 Weeks*. Judith lives in Herefordshire with her husband and two children.

Judith Wills
Slimmers'
Cookbook

Over 100 quick and easy
calorie-counted recipes

PIATKUS

Copyright © 1997 Judith Wills

First published in 1997 by
Judy Piatkus (Publishers) Ltd
5 Windmill Street, London W1P 1HF

This paperback edition published in 1999

Reprinted 1999

The moral right of the author has been asserted

*A catalogue record for this book is available from
the British Library*

ISBN 0-7499-1770-9 (hbk)
ISBN 0-7499-1881-0 (pbk)

Designed by Neil Sayer
Illustrations by Madeleine David
Photographs by Steve Baxter
Home economy by Oona van den Berg
Styling by Marian Price

Typeset by Wyvern 21 Ltd, Bristol
Printed and bound in Great Britain by
Bookcraft Ltd, Midsomer Norton

CONTENTS

INTRODUCTION

I'm a great believer in eating well. I sometimes think back ruefully to the days of my late teens and early to mid-twenties, when I could eat what I liked and as much as I liked without ever putting on an ounce. It was quite a shock to realise, in my late twenties and thirties, that I, like most of the rest of the population, had to watch what I ate in order to stay a reasonable shape – for, horrors, every time I put on a few pounds it would *always* end up around my middle. At one time, after the birth of my second child, I had 36-inch hips and a 32-inch waist! *You* try finding clothes to fit that kind of shape!

However, through my thirties, I also happened to be editing *Slimmer* magazine so, obviously, I had to set some kind of example. The problem was easy to define. If I were to get in shape and keep in shape, I needed to eat food that I could enjoy – and enough of it to satisfy my appetite. (Of course, I also needed to exercise – in fact, I took up swimming and rediscovered my bicycle.) No way was I going to live on 'diet food' – minuscule portions of the bland, the cardboardy, the tasteless. Nor was I going to spend hours producing 'cuisine minceur' type food, or special meals just for myself. Life is far too short and too busy for that sort of bother.

The food and menus in this book represent the kind of food that I discovered worked for me. Many of the recipes are not extremely low in fat, which will come as a surprise to many serial slimmers who have followed the 'no-fat' code for years. It is now recognised that we all need some fat in our diets, particularly of the mono- and polyunsaturated kinds, for good health. And I recognise that when cooking, a certain amount of fat – both occurring naturally in foods, and sometimes added during cooking – makes food interesting, tasty, palatable and enjoyable.

My philosophy on food, slimming and weight maintenance is as follows:

✦ You can eat more than you think you can and still lose weight.

✦ If you try to cut down too much and are too hard on yourself, cutting out all the things you like, you'll never stick to a diet. For this reason, you should be happy to lose weight quite slowly – better it comes off at 1 lb or even less a week than not at all, or than staying in the dieting 'yo-yo' trap.

✦ You have to feed yourself food you enjoy.

✦ You need to keep an open mind about ingredients, styles of food and cooking methods so that you don't get bored and can add taste and interest to your diet without too many calories.

✦ You have to know a little about healthy eating and apply some simple rules to your menu planning.

✦ And, yes, it really helps if you build more physical activity into your life.

By following this fairly mild philosophy, I have managed over the past few years to maintain a reasonable weight whilst still enjoying wine, three meals a day, eating out, holidays and entertaining. *You* can get slim and stay slim too, my way. I hope you enjoy the recipes, menus and ideas in this book as much as I have enjoyed producing them!

CHAPTER ONE

FAST, FABULOUS – AND HEALTHY!

Y ou like food but you want to lose weight. You *can* carry on enjoying your food *and* lose weight painlessly

✦ without hunger,
✦ without faddy eating,
✦ and without too much bother.

You can also, if you are cooking for other people, prepare meals as part of your slimming plan that everyone else will enjoy as well. Your partner, your children – don't for goodness' sake even think of doing separate meals for them. This book is all about *cooking food that everyone can enjoy*. Don't keep it to yourself.

SLIMMING THE EASY WAY

Chapters 3 to 11 of this book will provide you with enough recipes and meal ideas to see you through several months of slimming or more, and can form the basis of lifelong, enjoyable and healthy eating for weight maintenance. But first, in this chapter, we will take a look at the basic ideas behind the recipes.

Successful slimming depends on balancing your day's menus sensibly, rather than getting faddy about what foods you *must* and *mustn't* eat, so there is unlikely to have to be a revolution in your kitchen, any more than there will be one in your eating habits. Few of you will have to make drastic changes to how you are currently shopping and cooking. But if you're overweight, and you need to slim, there are bound to be things that you haven't been doing quite right. Let's look at them now.

To slim successfully you need to:

1 Cut out all unnecessary fat (particularly saturated fat) while leaving enough in your diet for good health and good taste
Every gram of fat that you eat contains 9 calories, whereas a gram of protein or carbohydrate contains only 4 calories. As fat is also very easy to eat, you can see why it is important for slimmers to cut down. Fat-cutting is easy to do by:

+ buying extra-lean cuts of meat, bacon, etc., and removing all visible fat and skin.
+ buying low-fat versions of high-fat products. You can get low-fat versions of very many items now, from yogurts to creams, cheeses, deserts, ice cream, salad dressings and many more.
+ replacing high-fat 'protein' foods on your plate with lower-fat or fat-free protein foods at least some of the time. Many foods that we, in our ignorance, consider to be 'protein' foods (important for muscle growth and repair and many other body functions), do, in fact, contain much more fat than they do protein; particularly some cuts of meat, and full-fat dairy produce. For example, 25 g (1 oz) Cheddar cheese contains 103 calories; 77 of those calories come from fat, and only 26 from protein. And the animal and dairy foods are also those highest in saturated fat, the type we should cut down on for good health. So, instead of these high-saturated-fat protein foods, use alternatives such as white fish, game, poultry (skin removed), tofu, Quorn or pulses as often as you can. This book is full of ways to turn lower-fat proteins into delicious meals.
+ cooking with the right utensils – heavy-based non-stick pans and griddles, a good grill, the microwave and steaming pans will all help you to use less fat in cooking.
+ taking care with how much fat you add to dishes through force of habit – for example, browning meat or onions in loads of butter isn't necessary, nor is stirring half a pot of double cream into your soup or adding butter as a garnish on vegetables.
+ using Fry Light, a cooking spray which combines olive oil with water. Used in combination with non-stick cooking pans, this is a useful product which reduces the amount of fat you use to brown onions, meat, etc. Find it alongside the oils on the supermarket shelf.
+ buying fewer ready-made food items, particularly bakery goods such as cakes and biscuits, and pastry goods such as pies, flans and sausage rolls.
+ limiting the amount of confectionery you eat, particularly chocolate and high-fat desserts.

If you follow these measures most of the time, you can then use a certain amount of oil and the occasional high-fat item in moderation in your cooking and still get or stay slim. You will also be able to eat the 'good for you' high-fat items such as nuts, seeds and avocados, without worrying too much about their high calorie content. *It makes sense to avoid fat calories that you don't need either for your health or for your tastebuds, and instead go for the 'healthy fats' and the fat that really will make a difference to the taste of what you eat* (see 'Healthy and Not-So-Healthy Fats', on page 7).

2 Only cut down a little on the 'complex carbohydrate foods'

Pasta, potatoes, pulses, rice, other grains, and breads are the foods that will help fill you up, provide much-needed fibre, vitamins and minerals, and will help keep hunger pangs at bay – particularly the pulses and pastas. (However, even people following a reduced-fat diet shouldn't go overboard on the carbohydrates – most of them are fairly calorie-rich and if you eat unlimited amounts you might not lose weight even if you are cutting down on your fats; see section 8, below, on exercising a degree of portion control.) But don't cut down at all on the amount of fresh or frozen fruits and vegetables and salad items on your plate. When we're slimming, most of us should actually eat *more* of these foods than we do.

3 Add flavour to your meals in low-calorie ways

Reduced-fat cooking need not be bland. Herbs, spices, sauces based on onions, tomatoes or other fruits or vegetables, chillies, soy and a myriad of other tasty ingredients brings fabulous flavour and style to your cooking. If you haven't been in the habit of experimenting with new flavours, this book will give you plenty of inspiration without stretching your time – or your culinary abilities – too much. Remember, if food tastes good, you won't miss high-calorie meals. If you don't miss high-calorie meals, you'll soon lose weight.

4 Keep a well-stocked storecupboard

If you get home from a hard day at work, you haven't had time to shop and there's nothing in stock at home but junk food, then that is what you will eat. Take time now and then to stock up the storecupboard with items from which you can produce a very quick and tasty meal. Here is a short list that you can build on as you work through the book: different shapes of dried pasta; a jar of pasta tomato sauce; a few cans of ready-cooked pulses such as lentils, red kidney beans, flageolets, butter beans, chickpeas (and of course baked beans) from which you can whiz up almost-instant soups, dips, pâtés and casseroles with a couple of ingredients from other cans or the freezer; canned tomatoes and tuna; a wide range of herbs, spices and seasoning sauces such as Tabasco (hot pepper), soy, Worcestershire and Thai fish sauce; cans of sweet peppers (pimientos), beansprouts, bamboo shoots and water chestnuts; quick-cook rice; dried Chinese and Italian mushrooms; dried fruits – and so on.

If you have a microwave, the freezer, of course, becomes an almost-instant storecupboard, too. Think of freezing fresh herbs in small quantities, of freezing grated half-fat strong cheese (a little goes a long way), of having home-made quick tomato sauce or soups on standby, frozen ready-prepared vegetables or ready-cooked rice, fillets of fish, prawns, etc. And, of course, if you use some of the recipes in this book which will freeze, and cook extra portions, you will have your own healthy meals ready and waiting for you. Which brings me to …

5 Plan ahead!

If you get home ravenous in the evening you could be eating within minutes, without resorting to two packets of crisps, if you have thought to put one of your homemade freezer meals out to thaw before you left home in the morning!

At weekends, if you have time, it is a great idea to plan the menus for the week ahead and then go shopping for what you need. Some meals can be cooked and frozen, others made in the morning and left in the fridge ready for the end of the working day; other meals, like most of those in this book, can be cooked when you get home and be ready in minutes. It takes less time to plan ahead than it does to muddle through – honestly! It is also less costly.

6 Don't be afraid to experiment with new recipes, cooking methods and ideas

As I said earlier, we aren't talking revolution here – but if you are to get slim and stay slim for the rest of your life, you need gradually to increase your repertoire of lower-calorie meals. This will mean keeping your eyes open for suitable recipes and not being afraid to try new ingredients, flavourings, and so on.

7 Eat when you are hungry

The worst mistake many people make when they are losing weight (or trying to) is to let themselves go hungry. Your body needs regular food – ideally, three small to medium meals a day and two small snacks – to be healthy and to give of its best. If you try to deny your body the food it needs, it will sooner or later rebel. You will give up the diet and probably have a good old binge and finish up fatter than you were in the first place.

Believe me – the way to permanent weight loss is to feed your body when it is hungry. But feed it good, healthy food. Give it variety. And *don't* put food in your mouth when you *aren't* hungry. Think of your body as a car; your stomach as the petrol tank. If the tank is full and you try to pour more fuel in, it's got nowhere to go. It's fuel wasted. In your body, the fuel is wasted as surplus fat. Don't do it. That's the nearest you'll get to a very strict rule in this book – but it's an important one to remember.

8 Exercise a degree of portion control

If you are overweight you have probably been piling more food on your plate at mealtimes than you really need to satisfy your hunger. You should get into the habit of giving yourself smaller portions. Sit and eat this smaller portion – slowly. If, when you have finished, you are still genuinely hungry (and I do say *genuinely* hungry), have a little bit more. Or have some fruit. After a week – only a week – you will find that if you try to eat the amount you used to, you will be satisfied before you can finish your plateful. I am not asking you to go hungry. Only to think about what you are doing when you eat. Portion control is simply an extension of the previous tip. You need to pay attention to what your body needs – give it that, and no more.

9 Lastly, learn a little about healthy eating and a little about the calorie content of the food you eat
This doesn't mean you have to become a walking encyclopaedia on nutrition, or look up how many calories there are in everything you eat. Far from it. Who's got the time or the incentive? But a few minutes spent on learning how to balance your menus for health (explained in 'Notes on Using the Recipes in this Book', pages 16–19) and on learning the 'traffic light' code to high, medium and low-calorie foods (pages 8–10), will help tremendously.

All the tips above will already have helped you to remember what healthy eating is all about – cutting down on certain fats and getting enough protein and carbohydrates, fresh fruit and vegetables. You'll find plenty more tips for slimming and healthy heating throughout this book, in the chapter introductions and recipe notes.

HEALTHY AND NOT-SO-HEALTHY FATS

A sensible fat intake to aim for in your diet is a maximum of around 30 per cent of your total calorie intake. For a woman on a maintenance diet, that would be equivalent to 63 g fat in total, only 21 g of which should be saturated. For a man it would be equivalent to 83 g in total, of which no more than 27 g should be saturated.

On a reduced-calorie diet, such as those recommended in this book, of around 1,400 calories a day for a woman or 1,600 for a man, the 30 per cent fat intake would be equivalent to 47 g total fat of which only 15 g should be saturated for a woman, and 53 g total fat (16 g saturated) for a man.

THE NOT-SO-HEALTHY FATS
Although we all need small amounts of saturated fat in our diet, to supply the fat-soluble vitamins A, D, E and K, (and to help our bodies absorb them), a high intake of saturated fat is linked to heart disease and stroke. Another type of fat, called trans fatty acids, is now thought to have a similar effect on us as saturated fat, and so the total saturated fat figures given above include these 'trans' fats. All the recipes in this book are low or fairly low in

saturated and trans fats, but here is a quick guide to the foods which supply both types of these fats in greatest quantity:

SATURATED FATS Butter, cream, traditional hard and creamy cheeses, whole milk and added-cream yogurts, whole milk, full-fat custards, fatty cuts of meat and game (such as farmed duck and goose), bacon and pork, sausages, meat products such as black pudding, pies, pastry, commercial desserts, lard and foods fried in lard or butter, coconut, chocolate, some mayonnaises.

TRANS FATS Many hard vegetable and/or fish-oil based margarines (look at the label to see if the ingredients list contains 'hydrogenated fats' – these are trans fats) and products made with these margarines, such as cakes, biscuits, pastries and desserts.

THE HEALTHY FATS

Other types of fats are polyunsaturated fats and mono-unsaturated fats. These are not 'bad for us' (unless we eat too much of them – they contain the same amount of calories as saturated and trans fats at 9 calories per gram, and so can contribute to a weight problem if we go overboard), as they are not linked with heart or circulatory disease. In fact, the consensus of opinion is that these fats, in moderation, are good for us – offering health benefits ranging from positive protection against heart disease to improving joint mobility and helping minimise skin complaints. So, whether on a slimming or a maintenance diet, these fats should make up at least two-thirds of our total fat intake. And it is important, on a slimming diet, *not* to try to reduce our intake of these unsaturated fats too much. Here's a short guide to where to find the 'good for you' fats in greatest quantities:

POLYUNSATURATED FATS Corn oil, sunflower oil, soya bean oil, safflower oil, evening primrose oil, most kinds of nuts and seeds, fish oil and oily fish.

MONO-UNSATURATED FATS Olive oil, groundnut (peanut) oil, rapeseed oil, avocados, nuts and seeds.

ESSENTIAL FATTY ACIDS Our bodies require small but regular amounts of two particular types of unsaturated fat, collectively called essential fatty acids: the omega-6 family (good sources of which are olive oil and sunflower oil) and the omega-3 family (oily fish, walnuts, flax seed/linseed, rapeseed oil and soya bean oil).

TRAFFIC-LIGHT GUIDE TO CALORIES

If you can fill your plate up with foods or recipe dishes that contain plenty of bulk without adding too many calories, then you will always find your hunger satisfied. Often, the foods highest in calories are those containing lots of fat! That is because, gram for gram, fat is over twice as calorific as either protein or carbohydrate. Often, the foods lowest in calories are those whose weight is made up largely of water or air. This is because water and air are calorie-free.

Usually, the *worst* foods to choose frequently when you are slimming are those which are both high in saturated fat and low in other nutrients such as vitamins, minerals, fibre and protein. These types of food are commonly called 'junk foods' and they are also usually the worst at filling you up, and certainly won't satisfy you for more than a little while.

Some high-fat, high-calorie foods aren't junk foods, though. Nuts, seeds and pure vegetable oils, for instance, are good for you in moderation and so, although they are high in calories, I have included them in the 'amber' section below.

This traffic-light guide is a very simple way of keeping a check on your calories for the rest of your life. Use it and you'll never actually have to *count* a calorie – or check out your fat intake – again.

RED FOODS

Treat these foods with extreme caution and eat and drink only very sparingly and/or very occasionally.

+ All foods high in saturated fat (see list above)
+ Alcohol (quite a few calories and no nutrients, but can be good for your heart in moderation)
+ Confectionery of all kinds (even if not high in fat, e.g. boiled sweets; confectionery is always high in calories and usually supplies very few or no nutrients)
+ Crisps and similar snack foods, including salted nuts

AMBER FOODS

Eat the following foods in moderate portions on a regular basis.

+ All foods listed under 'polyunsaturated fats' and 'mono-unsaturated fats' above
+ All kinds of fish and shellfish; eggs (limit to 7 a week maximum)
+ Reduced-fat dairy produce (e.g. semi-skimmed and skimmed milk, low-fat yogurts, fromage frais, low-fat and medium-low-fat cheeses)
+ Extra-lean meats, game (e.g. wild duck, pheasant, grouse, pigeon, rabbit), poultry (skin removed)
+ Vegetarian protein foods, e.g. all pulses and beans, low-fat burger mix, Quorn, tofu
+ Natural carbohydrates – potatoes, grains (including rice), pasta, bread, noodles.

These should be as 'unadulterated' as possible – e.g. wholegrain rice, wholewheat pasta, wholemeal bread, potatoes with their skins on, and so on

– at least some of the time, both for the extra fibre and for the vitamins and minerals the 'whole versions' will give you.

GREEN FOODS

Eat all you like of the following foods.

✦ Fresh and frozen fruits
✦ Fresh and frozen vegetables
✦ Salads
✦ Herbs and seasoning, with the exception of salt, which it might be wise to limit for your health's sake, especially if you have high blood pressure or any heart problems
✦ Water

If a food isn't listed in any category, read the label, if there is one, and use your common sense to decide whether or not it is a high-saturated-fat food. If it is, make it a 'red' food. If it isn't, put it in the 'amber' section.

Things like condiments and recipe ingredients, which you will use in small quantities only, aren't going to make a big difference to your overall calorie or fat intake, so don't worry too much about which category to put, say, anchovy essence into!

ARE YOU REALLY OVERWEIGHT?

Before beginning any of the diet plans or using the recipes in this book in order to slim, first you should ask yourself a simple question – Do I really need to lose weight?

Check out the Acceptable Weight Range Chart below and see if your current weight falls within the band for your height. If it is in the middle of your band or below, I don't think you should lose weight – you are fine as you are. Perhaps your body may need some toning and shaping through exercise, in which case consider a regular exercise class and some regular sport, such as swimming or cycling. If your weight is higher than the top weight listed for your height, then you should definitely lose some weight and begin regular exercise (gently at first, and do check with your doctor that you are fit to exercise).

If, like many of us, you find yourself falling just within the acceptable weight range for your height, but you still feel fat, then perhaps you could do with losing a little until your weight comes down to somewhere near the middle of the band. If you only have a little weight to lose – say 4.5 kg (10 lb) or less – be content to do it slowly and combine it with regular exercise.

Lastly, the older you are, the more realistic you should be about your own optimum weight – don't aim too low. As we get older, it is probably healthier to be *slightly* overweight than it is to be underweight.

Acceptable weight range chart
For men and Women

Height	Weight range	
	Lowest	Highest
1.52 m (5 ft 0 in)	46.3 kg (7 st 4 lb)	58.5 kg (9 st 3 lb)
1.55 m (5 ft 1 in)	47.6 kg (7 st 7 lb)	59.9 kg (9 st 6 lb)
1.57 m (5 ft 2 in)	49.4 kg (7 st 11 lb)	61.7 kg (9 st 10 lb)
1.6 m (5 ft 3 in)	50.8 kg (8 st 0 lb)	63.5 kg (10 st 0 lb)
1.63 m (5 ft 4 in)	52.6 kg (8 st 4 lb)	65.8 kg (10 st 5 lb)
1.65 m (5 ft 5 in)	54.4 kg (8 st 8 lb)	68 kg (10 st 10 lb)
1.68 m (5 ft 6 in)	56.2 kg (8 st 12 lb)	70.3 kg (11 st 1 lb)
1.7 m (5 ft 7 in)	58.1 kg (9 st 2 lb)	72.6 kg (11 st 6 lb)
1.73 m (5 ft 8 in)	59.9 kg (9 st 6 lb)	74.8 kg (11 st 11 lb)
1.75 m (5 ft 9 in)	61.7 kg (9 st 10 lb)	77.1 kg (12 st 2 lb)
1.78 m (5 ft 10 in)	63.5 kg (10 st 0 lb)	79.4 kg (12 st 7 lb)
1.8 m (5 ft 11 in)	65.8 kg (10 st 5 lb)	81.6 kg (12 st 12 lb)
1.83 m (6 ft 0 in)	68 kg (10 st 10 lb)	84.4 kg (13 st 4 lb)

The Importance of Exercise

If you are trying to lose body fat – and, indeed, once you have reached your target weight and are trying to maintain that weight – you must remember, it isn't just what you eat and don't eat that matters. A crucial factor in your success will be the amount, frequency and type of exercise that you take.

For your body to look in good shape, and for you to feel strong and supple, you need regular 'body conditioning' exercise to tone and strengthen your muscles and to keep your joints working smoothly. Toning exercises can take inches off your waist, for instance, and strength work can firm and tone your legs where your diet won't work at all.

Next, you also need to do cardio-vascular (aerobic) exercise such as brisk walking, cycling or an aerobics class, which will not only make your heart and lungs (and you!) fitter, but will also help burn off the calories in the food you eat, so helping your slimming or weight maintenance programme.

Aim to do body toning and conditioning exercises three times a week for at least 20 minutes and aerobic exercise three times a week for 30 minutes (preferably spacing all your sessions out evenly through the week).

OPPOSITE PAGE 10: Smoked Fish and Sweetcorn Chowder (page 26)

OPPOSITE: Thai Prawn Sizzle (page 73)

CHAPTER TWO

PLANNING YOUR DIET

Now it's time to convert all your knowledge into practical menus for the weeks ahead. At the end of this chapter you will find four week-long diet plans to help get you started. These are: a winter plan, a summer plan, a low-cost plan and a vegetarian plan, and each incorporates some of the recipes from this book.

Before long, though, you will want to plan your own daily eating, mixing and matching lunches and evening meals to suit yourself, and incorporating your own favourite snacks and meals along with my recipes. Later in this chapter, under the heading 'Notes on Using the Recipes in this Book', you will find information on balancing your diet and incorporating enough variety into your daily eating.

KEEPING HUNGER AT BAY

When slimming, women should aim to eat between 1,250 and 1,500 calories a day; men from 1,400 to 1,750 calories a day. As a general rule, the more overweight you are to start with, the more calories your slimming diet should contain. Your calorie intake should be split up into several 'segments' throughout the day, to help avoid hunger pangs, as I have done in the four diet plans. For example, if you are slimming on 1,400 calories a day, you could have:

Breakfast – 250 calories
Mid-morning snack – 50 calories
Lunch – 400 calories
Early supper – 500 calories
Snack – 50 calories
Extras (e.g. milk allowance, small treat) – 150 calories

Or you might prefer a bigger breakfast and lunch, and less in the evening, in which case a typical plan could be:

Breakfast – 350 calories
Mid-morning snack – 50 calories
Lunch – 500 calories
Late afternoon snack – 100 calories
Supper – 300 calories
Extras (e.g. milk allowance – 100 calories)

Diets shouldn't be written in stone – juggle yours to suit your own preferences. The only diet I would strongly advise you not to follow is the sort where you eat nothing all day except one meal in the evening. Try to eat 'little and often' – it's better on your digestive system and helps prevent hunger pangs and the dizziness and tiredness that dieters often complain about – brought about because they go for such long periods without eating and their blood sugar levels fall too low.

There are plenty of ideas for cooked meals and salads in the recipe chapters that follow, so I needn't give you any more ideas here, but here are some suggestions for breakfasts, between-meals snacks and quick and easy lunches to help you put together your own diet. There is also a list of treats – to be used with extreme caution!

BREAKFASTS

Ideally, breakfast should be a chance for you to eat a healthy, low-saturated-fat meal with a good balance of protein and carbohydrate plus a little unsaturated fat to keep you feeling full until your next snack or meal. It should always contain some fresh fruit or fruit juice (fruit not juice for preference), and/or some high-fibre dried fruits such as prunes, apricots, peaches or figs, which also supply lots of vitamins and minerals.

200 CALORIES AND MAXIMUM 2 g FAT Small tub natural low-fat Bio yogurt with 1 handful low-salt, low-sugar, luxury muesli and 1 portion chopped fresh fruit OR small tub natural low-fat fromage frais with 6 chopped no-need-to-soak dried stoned prunes, 1 chopped orange and 2 teaspoons chopped almonds sprinkled over.

250 CALORIES AND MAXIMUM 8 g FAT 1 kiwifruit, 1 small slice wholemeal toast with a very little low-fat spread and 1 small boiled egg and 1 medium banana OR ½ pink grapefruit, 25 g (1 oz) bran flakes or fruit and fibre cereal with skimmed milk to cover, 1 medium slice wholemeal toast with a little low-fat spread and low-sugar jam or Marmite, OR small tub natural low-fat Bio yogurt with 25 g (1 oz) low-salt, low-sugar luxury muesli and 1 portion chopped fresh fruit OR 2 Weetabix with skimmed milk to cover plus 1 apple and 1 small slice wholemeal toast with low-fat spread and Marmite or a very little low-sugar marmalade or jam OR ½ pink grapefruit, 125 g (4½ oz) baked beans on 1 slice wholemeal toast from a medium cut loaf with a very little low-fat spread.

300 CALORIES AND MAXIMUM 6 g FAT 50 g (2 oz) low-salt, low-sugar luxury muesli with 1 chopped apple and 1 chopped kiwifruit and skimmed milk to cover OR 1 orange, 175 g (6 oz) baked beans on one 40 g (1½ oz) slice wholemeal toast with a little low-fat spread.

350 CALORIES AND MAXIMUM 13 g FAT 1 medium poached egg, 3 tablespoons baked beans, 1 grilled extra-lean 25 g (1 oz) back bacon rasher, 4–5 mushrooms (microwaved or poached in a little stock, or seasoned and baked in foil), 1 halved and grilled tomato, 1 medium slice wholemeal bread with a little low-fat spread, 1 teaspoon low-sugar jam or marmalade.

BETWEEN-MEALS SNACKS

50 CALORIES AND MAXIMUM 2 g FAT EACH 1 piece fresh fruit (except banana) and 1–12 pieces if small, e.g. plum OR 1 average portion fresh berry fruits OR 1 rye crispbread with low-fat soft cheese and Marmite OR 1 average chunk cold boiled potato OR 1 diet yogurt or fromage frais.

100 CALORIES AND MAXIMUM 3 g FAT EACH Any two items from 50-calorie list OR 1 large banana OR 2 rye crispbreads, one spread with Marmite or low-sugar jam, the other with 1 heaped teaspoon hummus or low-fat soft cheese or tapenade OR 1 low-calorie can of soup and 1 crispbread OR small tub natural low-fat Bio yogurt with 1 teaspoon runny honey OR 1 small slice malt loaf with a little low-fat spread.

TREATS

If you are choosing treats as part of a diet you have designed yourself, choose one only if the fat and calorie content is within your day's allowance (approximately 47 g fat and 1400 calories per day for women, 53 g fat and 1600 calories for men). Maximum one a day.

50 CALORIES 1 reduced-fat digestive biscuit (2 g fat) or 1 rounded teaspoon butter (6 g fat) OR 1 tablespoon low-fat mayonnaise (4.5 g fat) OR 25 ml (1 fl oz) half-fat crème fraîche or half-fat cream (4 g fat) OR 2 teaspoons sugar or honey (no fat) OR 1 Jaffa Cake (1 g fat).

100 CALORIES Any two selections from the 50-calorie list OR 1 tablespoon French dressing (11 g fat) OR 15 g (½ oz) slice malt loaf (0.5 g fat) OR 125 ml (4½ fl oz) reduced-fat ice cream (3.5 g fat) OR tube of Polo mints (trace of fat) OR 1 Lo or Halo chocolate bar (4.7/3.8 g fat) OR 20 g bar Cadbury's Dairy Milk (6 g fat) OR 2 fingers Kit Kat (5.7 g fat) OR medium glass dry or medium wine (no fat) or 275 ml (½ pint) cider, beer or lager (no fat) or 1 double measure any spirit (no fat).

QUICK LUNCH IDEAS

300 CALORIES AND MAXIMUM 10 g FAT EACH Any of the 300-calorie breakfasts OR pitta bread filled with 100 g (3½ oz) tuna in brine (drained), a little oil-free French dressing and unlimited salad items OR any ready-made calorie-counted sandwich (from Boots, etc.) at 300 calories or less, but make sure it contains plenty of salad stuff (or add extra) OR sandwich of 2 slices wholemeal bread from a medium cut large loaf spread with a little low-fat salad cream or mayonnaise and filled with either 1 hard-boiled egg (sliced), or 100 g (3½ oz) tuna in brine (drained), or 50 g (2 oz) extra-lean ham or 75 g (3 oz) cottage cheese, plus unlimited salad items with any selection OR half a 568 ml (1 pint) carton fresh chilled soup (either lentil and vegetable, Tuscan bean, or winter vegetables and tomato), with a wholemeal roll and a piece of fresh fruit to follow.

400 CALORIES AND MAXIMUM 12 g FAT EACH Sandwich as above plus 1 large banana OR pitta bread filled with 50 g (2 oz) Feta or Halloumi cheese and salad, 1 orange, 1 diet yogurt or fromage frais OR 175 g (6 oz) baked beans on 40 g (1½ oz) slice wholemeal toast with a little low-fat spread and topped with 25 g (1 oz) grated half-fat Mozzarella cheese, heated until melting, 2 pieces fresh fruit or 1 large banana.

500 CALORIES AND MAXIMUM 15 g FAT EACH 1 can low-calorie soup plus 1 pitta bread filled with 2 tablespoons hummus plus unlimited salad and a little oil-free French dressing plus 1 diet fruit yogurt and 1 medium banana OR healthy ploughman's: 40 g (1½ oz) Brie or Edam, 75 g (3 oz) brown French bread with 2 teaspoons low-fat spread, unlimited salad items, 2–3 pickled onions, oil-free French dressing plus 1 apple and 1 large banana.

ENTERTAINING

If you like to have friends or family round for a meal, there is no reason to stop just because you're on a slimming programme. I would say that *all* the recipes in this book could be incorporated into a supper party without anyone realising they were eating 'slimmer's food' – as I said in the Introduction, you don't *need* to eat separate, peculiar or hunger-inducing 'rabbit' food in order to lose weight or to keep it off.

In chapter 3, there are plenty of starter ideas, in chapters 4–10 plenty of main-course ideas, and there are several easy dessert solutions in chapter 11.

Extra-hungry guests can feed on pre-meal nibbles (healthy ones like fresh nuts or crudités with tapenade or hummus) and can have more bread or second helpings if they insist – but it really shouldn't be necessary, and there is nothing worse than sending people home with uncomfortably full tums to a night of indigestion. Whatever you do, don't feel obliged to cook meals stuffed full of saturated fat. Ideal supper-party meals are salad starters, big bowls of pasta for a main course and a fruity dessert to finish. Theme your meal around a particular country and you can't go wrong. Here are some ideas for three-course meals you could serve using recipes in this book:

BRITISH Warm Goat's Cheese Salad; Venison Steaks in Red Wine; Creamed Plums

USA Smoked Fish and Sweetcorn Chowder; Prawn and Chicken Creole; Peach Melba

FRENCH Creamy Cheese Mousse; Tarragon Chicken; Poached Pears served with half-fat crème fraîche

ITALIAN Italian Bean and Pasta Soup; Mushroom and Artichoke Risotto; Tiramisu

EASTERN MEDITERRANEAN Chunky Aubergine Dipping Salad with crudités and slices of pitta; Lemony Lamb Kebabs served with couscous and a side salad; fresh figs and grapes with slices of grilled Halloumi cheese

ORIENTAL Egg Noodle and Crab Soup; Thai Pork with Almonds served with Thai fragrant rice, Grilled Bananas

VEGETARIAN Mushroom Pâté with melba toast; Bulghar Wheat Pilaff with Grilled Vegetables; Fruit-Filled Pancakes served with Greek yogurt

NOTES ON USING THE RECIPES IN THIS BOOK

All the recipes in the chapters that follow can form part of a healthy and balanced slimming or weight maintenance diet.

Although I have cut all *unnecessary* fat and calories from each recipe, as you flick through you might notice that the calorie and fat counts for different recipes in the same chapter vary quite considerably. This is because I want to give you as much choice as possible in designing your own daily eating – sometimes you will want a bigger lunch and a smaller evening meal; at other times you will feel like a light lunch and a larger evening meal. Again, you might want a smaller main course so you can have a dessert tonight, too, within your daily calorie allowance – and so on.

Eating to lose weight healthily means thinking not only about the calorie and fat content of any one particular meal, but *also about the overall BALANCE of your total diet*. First let's look at the recipes themselves and run through what you need to know in order to use them wisely in your daily diet.

Most recipes serve *two* people – because, according to my research, that is the number of people the majority of you want to serve when you cook a recipe dish, unless entertaining. But, obviously, you can easily double quantities for four, or sometimes even halve them to serve one, though that isn't always practical and some wastage might be involved. (A better bet if you're cooking for one is to make double quantities of suitable recipes and to freeze the surplus. Don't, whatever you do, eat it all in one go!) All recipes are quick to prepare – 30 minutes is the maximum time I allowed myself for preparation and cooking. In fact many recipes take less time than this. In many recipes, time is saved overall by using the time that one ingredient is cooking to prepare another. A simple logic, but one many cooks don't bother to use.

THE NUTRITION PANELS

At the start of each recipe a nutrition panel appears giving you the information you need to build that recipe into your slimming or maintenance diet.

CALORIES PER PORTION Decide how you want to split your day's calorie allowance up (see above) and find a recipe that fits in with the amount of calories you have allowed for that meal. There is a wide variety, with some meals as low as around 200 calories per portion, others going up to 600. If you have a higher-calorie evening meal one day, then you'll pick a lower-calorie lunch and breakfast, and so on.

TOTAL FAT PER PORTION This is given in grams. Check your total daily *maximum* recommended intake of fat on the chart below. You can then see at a glance how much of your daily total fat allowance you are using up on your chosen recipe, and how much fat you can eat during the rest of the day. If you choose an evening recipe that is higher in fat than most (though none in this book is actually high in fat), such as Broccoli and Egg Gratin (page 84) at 24 g, then you would choose a low-fat lunch, such as Smoked Fish and Sweetcorn Chowder (page 26) at 4 g fat. None of the suggested breakfasts on page 13, except the 350-calorie cooked breakfast, contains more than 6 g fat so if you choose one of those, this sample day's eating would now so far contain 34 g fat, leaving you enough 'spare' to cover two small snacks and even a 'treat' from the lists on page 14.

You don't *have* to eat the maximum daily fat allowance, but I wouldn't advise going *below* 30 g a day. Another good, quick method of checking whether you're getting about the right amount of fat in your diet is to make sure that no more than a third of the calories in any meal come from fat. So, for instance, if your main meal is 500 calories, one-third of that is 166 calories. Each gram of fat contains 9 calories, so the maximum fat content of that meal should be (166 divided by 9) 18 g. Obviously, some meals may go over this while others will be lower. There's no need to nit-pick but it is fun to check you're getting things right now and then.

When browsing through the recipe chapters that follow, you might find, when applying this 'one-third fat' criterion, that some of the recipes contain far more than one-third fat. For example, the Creamy Cheese Mousse (page 34) contains only 74 calories per portion but 6 g fat per portion, meaning that 54 of the calories are from fat (over 70 per cent). But, of course, you aren't going to eat the mousse on its own – it is meant to be served with toast or something similar, which would then bring the total fat content of the starter *as a whole* down to around one-third.

Similarly, the Lemony Lamb Kebabs on page 38 contain only 310 calories per portion but 14 g fat, which means that around 40 per cent of the recipe's calories are fat calories. But the dish is meant to be served with rice, couscous, or similar, bringing the calorie total up to around 500 for the meal, while the fat content stays the same, and 14 g fat in a 500-calorie meal is only 25 per cent fat. So you see, it is the *overall* balance of each meal that is important rather than the indivic ¬¹ components of it.

SATURATED FAT PER PORTION It's important for your health's sake to restrict the amount of saturated fat you eat, so I've given this as a separate figure. This isn't in addition to the total fat figure, of course. For example, the Italian Bean and Pasta Soup (page 27) contains 11 g total fat and 2 g saturated fat, so the remaining 9 g fat will be poly- or mono-unsaturated. Check the chart below to discover the maximum amount of saturated fat per day that you should be eating. Virtually all my recipes are very low in saturated fat anyway. If you want reminding of the foods that *are* high in saturated fat, check back to the list on page 8.

FATS – YOUR MAXIMUM DAILY ALLOWANCE AT A GLANCE

GRAMS OF FAT PER DAY MAXIMUM

	Men		Women	
	Total Fat	Sat Fat	Total Fat	Sat Fat
Average slimming diet (1,400 cals women/ 1,600 cals men)	53 g	16 g	47 g	15 g
Average maintenance diet (1,900 cals women/ 2,500 cals men)	83 g	27 g	63 g	21 g

PROTEIN PER PORTION The protein content of each dish is rated Low, Medium or High. Low means that the dish contains under 10 per cent of its total calories in the form of protein. Medium means that it contains between 10 and 15 per cent protein, and High means that it contains more than 15 per cent protein. We all need around 10–15 per cent of our total day's calories to be protein (some very active people need more). Again, as with the fat content, many of the savoury recipes in this book will appear to be high in protein, but these are almost always served with a carbohydrate, such as bread, potatoes, rice or pasta, which will bring the total protein content of the meal down and offer a good balance.

CARBOHYDRATE PER PORTION The carbohydrate content of each recipe is rated one, two or three stars. ★ means that the recipe contains under 35 per cent carbohydrate; ★★ means that it contains 35–50 per cent carbohydrate, and ★★★ means that it contains over 50 per cent carbohydrate. For good health, we need at least 50 per cent of our day's calorie intake to be in the form of carbohydrate such as bread, potatoes, rice, pasta, cereals and other grains. But, again, if a recipe appears to be low in carbohydrate, it is almost always a dish that is to be served with a carbohydrate accompaniment, bringing the total for the complete meal up to a higher carbohydrate rating.

FIBRE PER PORTION The fibre content of each dish is also rated one, two or three stars. ★ means that the recipe contains less than 2 g fibre per portion; ★★ means that it contains 2–6 g fibre per portion, and ★★★ means it contains over 6 g fibre per portion. We should aim for 18 g fibre a day in our diets. Often, the items recommended to accompany the recipes contain good amounts of fibre (especially if you choose whole grains rather than refined ones), and your daily breakfast should also contain plenty of fibre. Dried fruits, pulses, whole grains, fruits, vegetables, nuts and seeds all contain fibre. A fibre-rich diet will help you to feel full throughout the day and will help your digestive system.

VITAMINS AND MINERALS

The vitamin and mineral contents of the recipes aren't listed because *all* the recipes contain a wide variety of these 'micronutrients' in abundance – plenty of vitamins C, E, B group, A, D and beta-carotene, and plenty of iron, calcium, zinc, potassium and the other necessary minerals. Obviously, different recipes will contain these nutrients in differing amounts, just as they contain differing amounts of the major nutrients fat, protein and carbohydrate.

This is why on a healthy slimming diet, it is important to *get as wide a variety of foods* as you can. *Vary* your diet from day to day for maximum health. Don't live on a restricted selection of 'diet' foods (or indeed, of any food). Use the recipes in this book to form part of your balanced, varied, healthy diet – and you will get, and stay, slim for the rest of your life.

THE EATING PLANS

I've designed four easy-to-follow eating plans to help you lose weight – try them all if you like! Before you begin each one, here are a few notes:

CALORIE CONTENT Each eating plan provides from 1,300 or 1,400 to 1,600 calories per day, depending upon how many snacks/treats you allow yourself. If you have read all the information in chapter 1 and in the preceding sections of this chapter you will know which calorie level will suit your slimming campaign best. For example, if you have a lot of weight to lose, or are male, you should start on 1,600 calories a day. If you only have a little to lose, start on 1,300 calories a day – and if the weight comes off too quickly you can always go higher.

RECIPES In the plans, recipes for all the dishes in *italics* can be found in later chapters of this book. Check the index for page numbers.

'UNLIMITEDS' All the following foods and drinks are unlimited on your diet and you should make full use of them. Remember, particularly, to have plenty of water and leafy green vegetables or salads.

Drinks Water, mineral water, tea and coffee (but try to limit yourself to five weak cups a day, using milk from your daily allowance and artificial sweetener, unless you are taking your daily 'treat' as sugar), herbal teas, low-calorie squashes and diet drinks (but no more than two a day)

Eats Any leafy greens such as spinach and cabbage, and leafy salads and fresh herbs, spring onions, cucumber, pickled onions, oil-free French dressing, all fresh or dried herbs and spices, garlic, lemons, limes, chilli sauce, mustard, Worcestershire sauce, tomato purée

BETWEEN-MEALS SNACKS The amount of these you can have appears at the start of each eating plan. The Between-Meals Snacks and Treats lists are on page 14.

SUMMER SLIMMING PLAN
Basic diet: 1,300 calories a day This includes all meals listed below plus 275 ml (½ pint) skimmed milk for drinks, etc., and TWO 50-calorie snacks. Eat the two snacks as follows: one mid-morning, one late afternoon.

1,400 calories a day diet Add to the Basic 1,300-calorie diet ONE extra snack a day from the 100-calorie list OR ONE 100 calorie treat.

1,500 calories a day diet Add to the Basic 1,300 calorie-list ONE extra snack a day from the 100-calorie list PLUS ONE 100 calorie treat.

1,600 calories a day diet Add to the Basic 1,300-calorie diet ONE extra snack a day from the 100-calorie list PLUS ONE 100 calorie treat PLUS an additional 275 ml (½ pint) skimmed milk OR 125 ml (4½ fl oz) whole milk

DAY 1
Breakfast Choose one of the 250-calorie breakfasts from the list on page 13.
Lunch *Parma Salad*, I diet yogurt
Evening meal *Tagliatelle with Spinach and Mint Pesto*, 125 g (4½ oz) strawberries with I tablespoon half-fat Greek yogurt

DAY 2
Breakfast As Day I
Lunch *Chunky Aubergine Dipping Salad*, I pitta bread, Side salad
Evening meal *Tarragon Chicken*, 100 g (3½ oz) new potatoes, Green beans, I nectarine or peach

DAY 3
Breakfast As Day I
Lunch *Warm Goat's Cheese Salad*, 50 g (2 oz) French bread
Evening meal *Swordfish with Tomato Salsa*, Half portion *Rustic Vegetable Rosti*, 3 fresh apricots or plums

Day 4
Breakfast As Day 1
Lunch *Summer Vegetable and Mint Soup*, 1 wholemeal roll, 75 g (3 oz) cherries
Evening meal *Crab Cakes with Raita Sauce*, Side salad, *Summer Fruit Kebabs*

Day 5
Breakfast As Day 1
Lunch *Greek Pasta Salad*
Evening meal *Pepperoni Frittata*, Large side salad, *Rhubarb Fool*

Day 6
Breakfast As Day 1
Lunch *New York Pastrami Salad*, 1 orange
Evening meal *Summer Vegetable Gratin*, *Peach Melba*

Day 7
Breakfast As Day 1
Lunch *Salmon Salad with Pesto*, 1 small banana
Evening meal *Mushroom and Artichoke Risotto*, Green salad

WINTER SLIMMING PLAN
Basic diet: 1,400 calories a day (most people find they prefer a few extra calories in the winter). This includes all meals listed below PLUS 275 ml (½ pint) skimmed milk a day for drinks, etc., and ONE 50-calorie snack PLUS ONE 100-calorie snack. Eat the two snacks as follows: one mid-morning, one late afternoon.
1,500 calories a day diet Add to the Basic 1,400-calorie diet ONE extra 100-calorie snack OR ONE 100 calorie treat.
1,600 calories a day diet Add to the 1,500-calorie diet an additional 275 ml (½ pint) skimmed milk OR 125 ml (4½ fl oz) whole milk.

Day 1
Breakfast Choose one of the 250-calorie breakfasts from the list on page 13.
Lunch *French Bread Pepperoni Pizza*, Side salad
Evening meal *Bombay Vegetable Curry* with 50 g (2 oz) drained canned chick peas added, *Poached Pears* with 1 tablespoon low-fat Greek yogurt

Day 2
Breakfast As Day 1
Lunch *Smoked Fish and Sweetcorn Chowder*, 40 g (1½ oz) wholemeal bread, 1 satsuma
Evening meal *Venison Steaks in Red Wine*, 150 g (5½ oz) mashed potato (made with a little skimmed milk from allowance plus 1 teaspoon low-fat spread), Large portion green vegetable/s of choice

DAY 3
Breakfast As Day I
Lunch *Hot Bacon, Avocado and Mushroom Salad*, 50 g (2 oz) French bread
Evening meal *Bulghar Wheat Pilaff with Grilled Vegetables*, I medium banana

DAY 4
Breakfast As Day I
Lunch *Spicy Lentil Soup*, I small slice wholemeal bread, I kiwifruit or satsuma
Evening meal *Nasi Goreng*

DAY 5
Breakfast As Day I
Lunch *Couscous, Chickpea and Lamb Salad*, I orange
Evening meal *Spaghetti Puttanesca*, Green salad, *Fruit-filled Pancakes*

DAY 6
Breakfast As Day I
Lunch *Smoked Mackerel Pâté*, 2 medium-cut slices wholemeal bread, toasted, Watercress salad, Apple
Evening meal *Pork Stroganoff*, 40 g (1 ½ oz) medium egg noodles (dry weight), cooked according to pack instructions, Side salad

DAY 7
Breakfast As Day I
Lunch *Thai Prawn Salad*, I kiwifruit
Evening meal *Breast of Pheasant with Leek and Mushrooms*, 140 g (5½ oz) sweet potato, baked or boiled, I portion leafy greens of choice

VEGETARIAN SLIMMING PLAN
Basic diet: 1,300 calories a day This includes all the meals listed below PLUS 275 ml (½ pint) skimmed milk a day for drinks, etc., PLUS TWO 50-calorie snacks. Eat the two snacks as follows: one mid-morning, one late afternoon.
1,400 calories a day diet Add to the Basic 1,300-calorie diet ONE 100-calorie snack OR ONE 100 calorie treat.
1,500 calories a day diet Add to the Basic 1,300-calorie diet ONE 100-calorie snack OR ONE 100 calorie treat PLUS an additional 275 ml (½ pint) skimmed milk OR 125 ml (4½ fl oz) whole milk.
1,600 calories a day diet Add to the Basic 1,300-calorie diet ONE 100-calorie snack PLUS ONE treat PLUS an additional 275 ml (½ pint) skimmed milk OR 125 ml (4½ fl oz) whole milk.

DAY I
Breakfast Choose one of the 250-calorie breakfasts from the list on page 13.
Lunch Half a 450 ml (16 fl oz) carton fresh, chilled pea soup, *Mushroom Pâté*, 1½ slices wholemeal bread from a medium-cut loaf, toasted

Evening meal *Spinach and Cheese Burgers, Tomato Sauce*, I satsuma or kiwifruit

DAY 2
Breakfast As Day I
Lunch *Ciabatta Pizza*, I nectarine
Evening meal *Summer Vegetable Gratin* with 50 g (2 oz) diced Quorn or tofu added, *Creamed Plums*

DAY 3
Breakfast As Day I
Lunch *Potato Salad with Saffron and Eggs*, I medium banana
Evening meal *Penne with Stir-Fried Mediterranean Vegetables*, I apple

DAY 4
Breakfast As Day I
Lunch *Chunky Aubergine Dipping Salad*, I mini pitta bread, 2 plums
Evening meal *Thai Stuffed Omelette* (vegetarian option as listed in recipe notes), Large side salad, *Pineapple Flambé*

DAY 5
Breakfast As Day I
Lunch *Greek Pasta Salad*, I apple
Evening meal *Rustic Vegetable Rosti*, 50 g (2 oz) French bread, Side salad, I diet yogurt

DAY 6
Breakfast As Day I
Lunch 50 g (2 oz) hummus, I pitta bread, Tomato, black olive and onion salad, I medium banana
Evening meal *Stuffed Mushrooms*, Large green salad, *Fruit-Filled Pancakes* with I tablespoon half-fat Greek yogurt

DAY 7
Breakfast As Day I
Lunch *Tabbouleh with Egg*, Green salad
Evening meal *Rigatoni with Goat's Cheese and Aubergines*

BUDGET SLIMMING PLAN
Basic diet: 1,400 calories a day This includes all the meals listed below PLUS 275 ml (½ pint) skimmed milk a day for drinks, etc., PLUS ONE 50-calorie snack PLUS ONE 100-calorie snack. Eat the two snacks as follows: one mid-morning, one late afternoon.
1,500 calories a day diet Add to the Basic 1,400-calorie diet ONE extra 100-calorie snack OR ONE treat.
1,600 calories a day diet Add to the Basic 1,400-calorie diet ONE extra 100-calorie snack PLUS ONE treat.

DAY 1
Breakfast Choose one of the 250-calorie breakfasts from the list on page 13.
Lunch *Italian Bean and Pasta Soup*, 40 g (1½ oz) slice wholemeal bread,
1 kiwifruit
Evening meal *Bacon, Potato and Broccoli Gratin, Grilled Bananas*

DAY 2
Breakfast As Day 1
Lunch *Tuna and Tomato Pitta Pizza*, Green salad
Evening meal *Spicy Skewered Chicken*, 175 g (6 oz) boiled rice (cooked weight;
50 g/2 oz uncooked), Side salad, 1 apple

DAY 3
Breakfast As Day 1
Lunch *Tabbouleh with Egg*, 1 satsuma
Evening meal *Spaghetti Puttanesca*, Side salad, 1 diet yogurt

DAY 4
Breakfast As Day 1
Lunch *Spicy Lentil Soup*, 40 g (1½ oz) slice wholemeal bread, 1 apple or orange
Evening meal *Cod with a Crunchy Bacon Topping*, 75 g (3 oz) peas, *Rhubarb Fool*

DAY 5
Breakfast As Day 1
Lunch *Greek Pasta Salad*
Evening meal *Rabbit with Herbes de Provence*, 150 g (5½ oz) mashed potato
(made with a little skimmed milk from allowance plus 1 teaspoon low-fat
spread), White cabbage, 1 apple

DAY 6
Breakfast As Day 1
Lunch 150 g (5½ oz) baked beans, 2 slices wholemeal toast from a medium-
cut loaf, 1 teaspoon low-fat spread, 1 orange
Evening meal *Italian Meatballs in Tomato Sauce*, 150 g (5½ oz) couscous
(soaked weight; 40 g/1½ oz unsoaked), Green salad

DAY 7
Breakfast As Day 1
Lunch *Chicken and Lentil Salad*, 1 wholemeal roll, 1 small banana
Evening Meal *Eggs Florentine*, 40 g (1½ oz) wholemeal bread OR *Bombay
Curry*, 150 g (5½ oz) boiled rice (cooked weight; 40 g/1½ oz uncooked),
1 teaspoon mango chutney and 1 grilled chappati

CHAPTER THREE

SOUPS AND STARTERS

Homemade soups – and, indeed, many of the good-quality, healthy, chilled-counter soups you can now buy from the supermarket – are ideal food for slimmers. There is absolutely no need to add fattening cream or butter to your soup to make it taste delicious, as the recipes in this chapter show.

My favourite soups are those made by simmering masses of vegetables with various flavourings, which are then puréed (or part puréed) to give a thick, rich, tasty and *large* bowlful that will satisfy your appetite and keep it satisfied for hours, as well as providing you with a large chunk of your daily vitamins. The addition of a protein such as lentils or beans gives you a compete meal in a bowl.

Use the recipes here to get you started – soup making really *is* very easy – then make up some ideas of your own. For instance, dice leeks, potatoes and onion and simmer in vegetable or chicken stock, then purée, to make a creamy yet healthy vichyssoise to serve hot or cold. Or try carrots simmered in stock with passata and seasoning, then puréed, for a carrot and tomato soup that almost makes itself.

Soups always make a great cool-weather lunch with some toast or crunchy bread – take them to work with you in a wide-necked flask as a change from sandwiches.

I've included a small selection of starters in this chapter which can also be used as lunchtime snacks – mostly pâtés and dips which, again, are very easy to make. Shop-bought pâtés and dips are often very high in fat so it is better to make your own when you can.

Smoked Fish and Sweetcorn Chowder

<u>SERVES 2</u>

CALORIES PER PORTION: 282	PROTEIN: HIGH
TOTAL FAT PER PORTION: 4 g	CARBOHYDRATE: ★★
SATURATED FAT PER PORTION: 1.5 g	FIBRE: ★★

THIS hearty American-style soup makes a good lunch, with some crusty wholemeal French bread to dip into the bowl!

4 large spring onions, finely sliced	100 g (3½ oz) unsmoked haddock (or other white
1 medium old potato (about 225 g/8 oz), cut into	fish) fillet, diced
2 cm (¾ inch) cubes	75 g (3 oz) frozen sweetcorn kernels
1 medium stick celery, chopped	200 ml (7 fl oz) semi-skimmed milk
200 ml (7 fl oz) fish stock	1 rounded teaspoon cornflour mixed with
2 sprigs fresh thyme	1 tablespoon cold water or stock
2 rashers extra-lean smoked bacon (about 50 g/	1 rounded tablespoon (20 ml) half-fat Greek yogurt
2 oz), diced	(optional)
100 g (3½ oz) undyed (if possible) smoked haddock	freshly ground white pepper
fillet, diced	fresh herbs to garnish, e.g. dill, tarragon, thyme

Simmer the onions, potato and celery in the stock in a covered saucepan with the thyme for 15 minutes. Meanwhile, heat the bacon in a small non-stick frying pan so that it cooks in its own fat, stirring occasionally, until golden and crisp. Pat the bacon pieces between two sheets of absorbent kitchen paper to remove any surplus fat.

Add the fish and sweetcorn to the saucepan and simmer gently for 5 minutes. Add the milk and simmer for a few minutes. Add the cornflour mixture and simmer for 1–2 minutes, stirring. Before serving, stir in the yogurt, if using, and season with pepper. Serve the soup in bowls, garnished with the bacon pieces and fresh herbs.

NOTES AND TIPS

✦ *Because the smoked fish and the bacon are quite salty I haven't added any extra salt. Taste the chowder before serving, and if it isn't salty enough for your taste, add a little more.*

✦ *The chowder is nice with other types of fish, too – for a luxurious touch you could substitute prawns for half the smoked fish, and monkfish for the fresh haddock. But to be correct, whatever your mix, you should use 50 per cent smoked or salty fish and 50 per cent unsmoked white fish.*

Italian Bean and Pasta Soup

SERVES 2

CALORIES PER PORTION: 275	PROTEIN: HIGH
TOTAL FAT PER PORTION: 11 g	CARBOHYDRATE: ★★
SATURATED FAT PER PORTION: 2 g	FIBRE: ★★

This is a lovely soup for cooler days, with a real bite to it. It will keep the hunger pangs at bay for hours, as both pasta and flageolet beans are slow to release their energy.

50 g (2 oz) dried pasta shapes of choice, preferably wholewheat	dash of Tabasco (hot pepper) sauce
	200 ml (7 fl oz) vegetable stock
1 small onion (about 100 g/3½ oz), finely chopped	100 g (3½ oz) canned flageolet beans, drained
1 medium clove garlic, finely chopped	salt and freshly ground black pepper
2 teaspoons olive oil	a few basil leaves (optional)
200 g (7 oz) can chopped tomatoes with herbs	1 tablespoon ready-made fresh pesto sauce

Heat a saucepan of lightly salted water and cook the pasta shapes for 5 minutes or until part-cooked. While the pasta is cooking, stir-fry the onion and garlic in the oil in a sauté pan for about 5 minutes or until soft and just turning golden. Drain the pasta.

Add the tomatoes and Tabasco to the sauté pan and stir for 1 minute, then add the stock and stir again. Add the pasta, beans and seasoning, and simmer gently for 10 minutes. Before serving, stir in the fresh basil leaves, if using, and the pesto sauce (but don't allow the soup to cook once the sauce has been added or its fresh flavour will immediately be lost).

NOTES AND TIPS
✦ *A sprinkling of grated Parmesan or Pecorino cheese over the soup just before serving makes it even nicer – 2 rounded teaspoons adds 25 calories and about 2 g fat.*
✦ *You can use other beans if you like – butter beans are nice – but don't use firmer varieties such as soya beans or black beans.*

Summer Vegetable and Mint Soup

<u>SERVES 2</u>

CALORIES PER PORTION: 205	PROTEIN: MEDIUM
TOTAL FAT PER PORTION: 11.5 g	CARBOHYDRATE: ★★
SATURATED FAT PER PORTION: 5 g	FIBRE: ★★

A wonderful all-rounder soup, simple to make for lunch yet classy enough for a dinner party.

2 teaspoons butter	75 g (3 oz) broccoli florets
2 teaspoons corn oil	1–2 tablespoons chopped fresh mint
2 leeks, thinly sliced and rinsed	salt and freshly ground black pepper
200 g (7 oz) new potatoes scraped and cut into 2 cm (¾ inch) cubes	4 teaspoons half-fat crème fraîche
	mint leaves to garnish
400 ml (¾ pint) vegetable or chicken stock	

Heat the butter and oil in a saucepan and sauté the leeks, stirring now and then, for 2–3 minutes. Add the potatoes and stock, and simmer for 10 minutes, then add the broccoli and simmer for a further 5 minutes. Cool the soup slightly, then purée in a blender.

Return the soup to the pan, stir in the mint and seasoning and reheat gently. To serve, swirl in the crème fraîche and garnish with mint leaves.

NOTES AND TIPS

✦ *This soup freezes quite well – freeze before adding the mint and crème fraîche.*

✦ *The soup works best with top-quality fresh vegetables; it pays to choose a tasty new potato such as Jersey Royal or Charlotte, and the broccoli needs to be very deep green and firm.*

Spicy Lentil Soup

SERVES 2

CALORIES PER PORTION: 240	PROTEIN: HIGH
TOTAL FAT PER PORTION: 7g	CARBOHYDRATE: ★★★
SATURATED FAT PER PORTION: 1g	FIBRE: ★★

LENTIL soup is the easiest thing in the world to make, and if you use red lentils, they will cook very quickly, too. An ideal soup for a chilly winter day and, again, *very* good at keeping hunger pangs at bay, long-term.

1 medium onion, finely chopped	100g (3½oz) red lentils, washed
1 tablespoon corn or olive oil	salt and freshly ground black pepper
pinch each of ground cinnamon and grated nutmeg	flat-leaved parsley or coriander to garnish
300ml (11fl oz) vegetable or ham stock	

Stir-fry the onion in the oil in a saucepan for 3 minutes or until the onion is soft and just turning golden. Stir in the spices, then add the stock and lentils, cover, and simmer gently for about 20 minutes or until the lentils are soft (check as the cooking time will vary slightly according to the age of the lentils). Add the seasoning, cool the soup slightly, and purée in a blender. Return to the pan and reheat. Check the seasoning and serve, garnished with parsley or coriander.

NOTES AND TIPS
✦ *It is important to use a good-flavoured stock for this soup.*
✦ *You could use brown or green lentils but they might take a little longer to cook.*

Egg Noodle and Crab Soup

SERVES 2

CALORIES PER PORTION: 240	PROTEIN: HIGH
TOTAL FAT PER PORTION: 11g	CARBOHYDRATE: ★★
SATURATED FAT PER PORTION: 4g	FIBRE: ★★

CHINESE-STYLE soups are easy to fling together yet quite impressive. Crab is a very crafty ingredient – the local market at my favourite seaside resort, Tenby, sells large, ready-dressed crabs for around £2 each. I sometimes use the white meat in this recipe, and make a pâté with the dark meat.

50 g (2 oz) egg thread noodles	400 ml (¾ pint) chicken stock
2 teaspoons groundnut (peanut) or sesame oil	1 tablespoon dry sherry or sake (optional)
2 teaspoons butter	white meat from one medium dressed crab, lightly
4 spring onions, trimmed and halved lengthways	separated with a fork
1 medium stick celery, cut into 4 cm (1¾ inch)	dash of Tabasco (hot pepper) sauce
julienne strips	salt and freshly ground black pepper
1 medium carrot, cut into 4 cm (1¾ inch) strips	fresh herbs to garnish

Cook the noodles in a pan of simmering water for 3 minutes or as instructed on the packet. Drain and cover with cold water until needed. Meanwhile, gently heat the oil and butter in a non-stick sauté pan, add the vegetables, cover, and cook gently for 5 minutes. Add the stock and sherry or sake, if using, and simmer for 5 minutes more, then add the crab meat, drained noodles, Tabasco and seasoning, and reheat. Taste and adjust the seasoning if necessary, then serve straight away with a herb garnish.

NOTES AND TIPS

✦ *For a heartier soup you could make a two-egg omelette, slice it into strips and add it to the soup with the crab meat. This would add 80 calories and 6g fat per portion.*

✦ *I have used the very fine egg 'thread' noodles, which take virtually no time to cook. If you can't get them, you could use medium egg noodles which are thicker and take about 6 minutes to cook. The taste is the same, but the finer noodles do look prettier and are easier to eat in this recipe. Whichever you use, read the pack instructions for cooking as they do vary; sometimes you need only soak the noodles for a few minutes in just-boiled water.*

Mushroom Pâte

SERVES 2–6

CALORIES PER PORTION: 130 (2 SERVINGS); 43 (6 SERVINGS) TOTAL FAT PER PORTION: 9 g (2 SERVINGS); 3 g (6 SERVINGS)	SATURATED FAT PER PORTION: 2 g (2 SERVINGS); 1 g (6 SERVINGS) PROTEIN: HIGH CARBOHYDRATE: ★ FIBRE: ★

THIS quick pâté can be turned into a dip if you thin it with a little skimmed milk or vegetable stock.

200 g (7 oz) brown-cap mushrooms or other firm, tasty, medium-sized mushrooms	1 tablespoon lemon juice
1 large stick celery	100 g (3½ oz) low-fat soft cheese
1 tablespoon olive oil	1 teaspoon Thai fish sauce or anchovy paste (see note)
1 small clove garlic, crushed	salt and freshly ground black pepper

Remove the stalks from the mushrooms, dry them on absorbent kitchen paper if necessary and chop them finely with a large, good-quality knife. Chop the celery similarly, discarding any stringy bits.

Heat the olive oil in a medium non-stick frying pan and fry the mushrooms and celery over a medium high heat, stirring frequently. After 5 minutes, add the garlic and stir well. Continue frying for a few minutes more until the mushrooms are cooked but not soggy. (If you have too much liquid you have used too small a pan!) Add the lemon juice and stir, then allow to cool for a minute.

Put the mushroom mixture into a blender with the cheese, fish sauce or paste and seasoning, and blend for a few seconds until you have a smooth pâté. (Pulse the blender a few times for best results instead of keeping it running constantly.) Check the seasoning and serve.

NOTES AND TIPS

✦ *Fish sauce comes in bottles and is available in most supermarkets.*

✦ *For a firmer pâté, you could add a tablespoon or two of dry breadcrumbs – useful if you find the blended mixture too runny.*

✦ *As with Chunky Aubergine Dipping Salad (page 32), this pâté will serve from two to six or more, depending upon how you use it.*

Chunky Aubergine Dipping Salad

SERVES 2–6

CALORIES PER PORTION: 195 (2 SERVINGS); 65 (6 SERVINGS) TOTAL FAT PER PORTION: 18g (2 SERVINGS); 6g (6 SERVINGS)	SATURATED FAT PER PORTION: 3g (2 SERVINGS); 1g (6 SERVINGS) PROTEIN: LOW CARBOHYDRATE: ★ FIBRE: ★★

I MADE this dip-cum-salad-cum-spread recently, and spooned it on to large homemade croûtons (see note) as part of a party buffet and it seemed nearly everyone wanted the recipe. As with so many incredibly more-ish dishes, it couldn't be easier to make.

2 medium aubergines (each weighing about 200g/ 7oz)	1 tablespoon lemon juice
salt and freshly ground black pepper	2 spring onions, finely chopped
2 tablespoons olive oil	1 tablespoon finely chopped fresh mint
1 large or 2 small cloves garlic, crushed	2 rounded teaspoons tahini paste (see note)

Put the grill on to heat up and boil a kettleful of water. Top and tail the aubergines and cut them into 1 cm (½ inch) thick rounds. Halve each round. Put the boiling water into a saucepan over high heat, add a little salt and, when the water has come back to the boil, add the aubergine pieces and blanch them for 2–3 minutes. Drain and pat dry on absorbent kitchen paper.

Brush a baking sheet with a quarter of the olive oil, lay the aubergine pieces on top and brush them with another quarter of the oil. Grill fairly near the heat for 5 minutes, then turn the chunks over and grill for another few minutes, until the aubergine is soft and flecked with brown. Tip the chunks on to a chopping board and chop into small pieces, using a good-quality, heavy knife.

In a bowl, mix the aubergine, garlic, lemon juice, seasoning, onions and mint, stirring well. Add the remaining olive oil and the tahini paste, and mix again. Check the seasoning and serve.

NOTES AND TIPS
✦ *The recipe will serve two hungry people for lunch with crusty bread or pitta and crudités; or is enough for a bowlful of party dip for several people; or will serve 4–6 as a starter; or will top approximately 16 homemade croûtons (see below).*

✦ *To make croûtons, cut the crusts off the slices from a medium-sized wholemeal loaf and cut each slice into four squares. Brush each square lightly with olive oil and bake in the oven at 180°C/350°F/Gas Mark 4 for approximately 20 minutes or until the croûtons are crisp and golden. (Watch them for the last few minutes as they burn very quickly once ready – as I know to my cost!)*

✦ *Tahini paste is made from sesame seeds and is available in most supermarkets and all health food shops.*

✦ *A few pitted black olives, chopped, make a good garnish for this salad.*

✦ *Use chopped parsley instead of mint for a change.*

Smoked Mackerel Pâté

SERVES 4–6

CALORIES PER PORTION:	SATURATED FAT PER PORTION:
155 (2 SERVINGS); 104 (6 SERVINGS)	3 g (2 SERVINGS); 2 g (6 SERVINGS)
TOTAL FAT PER PORTION:	PROTEIN: HIGH
12 g (2 SERVINGS); 8 g (6 SERVINGS)	CARBOHYDRATE: ★
	FIBRE: ★

MACKEREL is high in the healthy omega-3 fish oils and this recipe is a tasty way to eat it, especially if you find the fish itself a bit too strong when served as a main meal. Again, the pâté can be thinned with skimmed milk to turn it into a dip or spread.

150 g (5½ oz) smoked mackerel fillet	2 teaspoons lemon juice
100 g (3½ oz) 0% fat fromage frais	salt and freshly ground black pepper
2 teaspoons creamed horseradish	1 tablespoon finely chopped fresh parsley

In a bowl, flake the mackerel fillet and combine well with the remaining ingredients. Check the seasoning and chill until required.

NOTES AND TIPS

✦ *This pâté is quite rich so you won't need as much of it per portion as the other pâtés in this chapter.*

✦ *If you like spicy food you could use the peppered variety of smoked mackerel instead. Another alternative is to use smoked trout, which is lower in omega-3s, fat and calories.*

Creamy Cheese Mousse

<u>SERVES 4</u>

CALORIES PER PORTION: 74	PROTEIN: HIGH
TOTAL FAT PER PORTION: 6 g	CARBOHYDRATE: ★
SATURATED FAT PER PORTION: 3 g	FIBRE: ★

A FRIEND served this as a starter and gave me the recipe, knowing how much I rely on things that an eight-year-old could make but which taste delicious. Compared with most savoury mousses and, indeed, any starter based on cheese, it is also low in calories. What could be better? Even if you think the ingredients sound weird, give it a go. It's not worth making two portions, so the recipe is for four, but it will freeze.

125 g (4½ oz) reduced-fat cream cheese, e.g. Light Philadelphia	½ teaspoon mild curry powder
	1 teaspoon tomato purée
125 g (4½ oz) canned beef consommé	2 teaspoons light mayonnaise
1 cm (½ inch) garlic purée (from a tube) or 1 very small garlic clove, chopped	fresh herbs to garnish

Put all the ingredients, except the herbs, in a blender and blend for a short while until smooth. Pour the mixture into individual pots and chill in a very cold fridge until set. Before serving, garnish with fresh herbs.

NOTES AND TIPS

✦ *Serve with wholemeal toast and/or crudités. Add approximately 60 calories for a small slice of toast.*

Warm Goat's Cheese Salad

SERVES 2

CALORIES PER PORTION: 226	PROTEIN: HIGH
TOTAL FAT PER PORTION: 19g	CARBOHYDRATE: ★
SATURATED FAT PER PORTION: 8g	FIBRE: ★

AN ideal lunch snack for cheese lovers containing far less saturated fat than a traditional ploughman's – or an impressive dinner-party starter which never goes wrong.

one 100g (3½oz) goat's cheese	I tablespoon French dressing (see note)
mixed salad leaves (about 50g/2oz)	2 teaspoons pine nuts
a few sprigs watercress	2 teaspoons balsamic vinegar
4 cherry tomatoes *or* 4 red apple slices, tossed in lemon juice	

Preheat the grill. Cut the goat's cheese in half so that each person has a round. Put each cheese half on the grill pan with the crust side on the bottom and the soft inner side at the top, and grill under a high heat for 3–5 minutes or until the cheese is flecked golden and bubbling.

While the cheese is cooking, arrange the salad leaves, watercress and tomatoes around the edge of two breakfast-size plates or shallow bowls, and sprinkle the French dressing and pine nuts over them. When the cheese halves are just cooked, transfer them to the salad plates using a metal spatula. Drizzle a teaspoon of balsamic vinegar over each and serve immediately.

NOTES AND TIPS

✦ *Make your own French dressing – it is much nicer than the bottled varieties. In a screw-topped jar, shake together three parts good olive oil to one part red wine vinegar with a little caster sugar, dry mustard powder, salt and black pepper. Taste and adjust the seasoning. One tablespoon will be approximately 100 calories with 11g fat.*

✦ *Serve the goat's cheeses with thin slices of wholemeal toast as a starter, or crusty French bread as a snack or lunch.*

CHAPTER FOUR

MEAT

Most people I know seem to think of meat as one of the first foods to cut out of a slimming diet, because 'it's fatty and fattening'. It is also often thought of as an 'unhealthy' food and perceived to have a high saturated fat content. On both counts, this is unfair to meat.

Yes, the fattier cuts, such as shoulder of lamb and belly of pork, sausages and many meat products, such as pork pies, *are* very fatty, calorific foods, but lean cuts of meat such as mince with a fat content of less than 10 per cent, lamb steaks, and tenderloin of pork are quite low in fat and calories – lower in both than many other sources of protein, such as Edam cheese or chicken eaten with the skin on! For example, 100 g (3½ oz) pork tenderloin contains 144 calories and 7.2 g fat, while 100 g (3½ oz) Edam has 304 calories and 22.8 g fat; chicken has 228 calories per 100 g (3½ oz), unless skinned, and 16.8 g fat. And, surprisingly, the fat content of meat is by no means *all* saturated. Most red meats contain no more than 50 per cent saturated fat; the rest is mono- or polyunsaturated.

Meat is also a good source of iron and B vitamins (and, of course, protein), so if you enjoy it, there is no reason not to include it in your slimming diet. Simply watch your portion sizes and think of meat as part of your complete meal, rather than the star of it. Always go for lean, or trim off all visible fat from the meat you buy, and always add plenty of carbohydrate.

If you haven't got more than a couple of minutes to spare, here are some quick ideas:

★ Toss cubes of pork, lamb or beef in olive oil, then sprinkle with chopped parsley and rosemary before threading on to kebab skewers or sticks and grilling.
★ Brush lamb steaks with olive oil and runny honey and sprinkle with chopped mint and garlic before grilling.
★ Sprinkle paprika and lemon juice on to sliced pork tenderloins before grilling or dry-frying.

Lamb, Potato and Mint Compote

<u>SERVES 2</u>

CALORIES PER PORTION: 478	PROTEIN: HIGH
TOTAL FAT PER PORTION: 18g	CARBOHYDRATE: ★
SATURATED FAT PER PORTION: 5g	FIBRE: ★★★

YOU will need leftover roast lamb and cooked new potatoes for this recipe, and leftover mint sauce would also help. In other words, it's a perfect Monday supper after a Sunday roast. But if you have no leftover potatoes or mint sauce you can still make the recipe – just – in 30 minutes.

150 g (5½ oz) green beans, topped and tailed	200 g (7 oz) cooked lean leg of lamb, cut into bite-sized pieces
1 medium courgette, sliced into thin rounds	
1 tablespoon olive oil	4 tablespoons traditional homemade mint sauce (see note)
1 clove garlic, chopped	
4–6 spring onions, chopped	salt and freshly ground black pepper
300 g (11 oz) cooked new potatoes, sliced unless tiny (see note)	2 tablespoons half-fat Greek yogurt
	1 pack baby spinach leaves or lamb's lettuce to serve

Bring a small pan of lightly salted water to the boil. Add the green beans and courgettes, and blanch for 2 minutes. Drain and pat dry on absorbent kitchen paper. Heat the oil in a large non-stick or heavy stainless-steel sauté pan and stir-fry the beans and courgette with the garlic, spring onions and potatoes for 2 minutes over a medium high heat. Add the lamb and stir for 1 minute to heat through. Pour the mint sauce over and stir, then add some seasoning and finally stir in the yogurt. Serve immediately on the leaves.

NOTES AND TIPS

✦ *If you have no cooked potatoes, put them on to boil before you do anything else. When nearly cooked, you can blanch the beans and courgettes and continue as above.*

✦ *To make traditional mint sauce, put 3 tablespoons finely chopped mint in a small bowl with 2 teaspoons sugar. Pour over a very little boiling water to just cover, stir and leave until the sugar has dissolved. Stir in 2 tablespoons malt or red wine vinegar. Leave in a warm place for the flavours to develop. If you have no mint sauce already made, you should make it while the potatoes are boiling, or if you have cooked potatoes but no mint sauce, make it before you begin the recipe above.*

Lemony Lamb Kebabs

<u>SERVES 2</u>

CALORIES PER PORTION: 310	PROTEIN: HIGH
TOTAL FAT PER PORTION: 14g	CARBOHYDRATE: ★
SATURATED FAT PER PORTION: 1g	FIBRE: ★★

AS I mentioned on page 36, the best way to eat meat without guilt when you are trying to watch your weight, is to use recipes where the meat is bulked out with other low-fat ingredients. These kebabs are a typical example.

200g (7oz) lean lamb fillet, e.g. leg	2 small peppers (any combination of red, yellow and orange)
1 unwaxed organic lemon (see note)	
1 large clove garlic, crushed	100g (3½oz) ready-prepared polenta (see note)
1 tablespoon olive oil	**TO SERVE**
salt and freshly ground black pepper	2 tablespoons natural low-fat Bio yogurt
1 good sprig fresh rosemary or 1 teaspoon dried	2 tablespoons diced cucumber
2 good sprigs fresh thyme or 2 teaspoons dried	lemon slices to garnish

Cut the lamb into 2–2.5 cm (³⁄₄–1 inch) cubes and place in a shallow bowl. Grate 2 teaspoons rind (no white pith) from the lemon, using a fine grater, and add to the bowl. Halve the lemon, squeeze out the juice, and add this to the bowl with the garlic, oil, seasoning and herbs. (If using fresh herbs, de-stalk them and discard the stalks.) Stir everything well. At this stage, if you have time, leave in a cool place, covered, to marinate. (Up to 12 hours will be fine, so, if you plan ahead, you could prepare this far in the morning and finish the dish off in the evening, for instance.) If you have no time to marinate the meat, don't worry – proceed.

Preheat the grill. Halve and de-seed the peppers and then cut each half into two, or possibly three, squarish pieces. Cut the polenta into slices about 1 cm (½ inch) thick. Thread the meat, peppers and polenta prettily on to four small or two large skewers (or bamboo satay sticks pre-soaked in water for 30 minutes). Grill for 4–5 minutes on one side, then turn, baste with the marinade juices, and grill for 3–4 minutes on the other side until everything is starting to char slightly. Serve the kebabs with a sauce made by mixing the yogurt and cucumber. Garnish with lemon slices.

NOTES AND TIPS

✦ *As this recipe requires you to use the lemon rind, it is best to use a lemon that hasn't been sprayed with chemicals or waxed.*

✦ *Serve with rice, couscous, noodles or any grain of your choice. An average tablespoon of cooked grain adds approximately 20 calories and little fat.*

✦ *The kebabs can also be made using lean fillet of pork or even organic beef.*

✦ *Ready-prepared polenta is available in good supermarkets.*

Lamb Koftas with Pitta

SERVES 2

CALORIES PER PORTION: 500	PROTEIN: HIGH
TOTAL FAT PER PORTION: 14g	CARBOHYDRATE: ★★
SATURATED FAT PER PORTION: 2g	FIBRE: ★★

HERE'S another lamb recipe containing mint and yogurt – but completely different in style from the roast lamb compote on page 37.

200g (7oz) minced lean lamb fillet	I small egg, beaten
25g (I oz) dry white breadcrumbs (see note)	100ml (3½fl oz) half-fat Greek yogurt
I small onion, finely chopped	2 round wholemeal pitta breads
I small clove garlic, finely chopped	chopped crisp lettuce leaves
I½ tablespoons finely chopped fresh mint	chopped cucumber
salt and freshly ground black pepper	I tomato, chopped

Preheat the grill. In a bowl, combine the first six ingredients (but saving ½ tablespoon of the mint for later), then add enough egg (you might not need it all) to bind them together. Using your hands, form into eight small sausage shapes and thread two (lengthways) on to each of four skewers.

Grill the koftas for 5 minutes, then turn and grill on the other side for a few minutes more until golden and sizzling. While they are cooking, mix the remaining chopped mint with the yogurt. Fill the pittas with the yogurt dressing and salad. Add the koftas (removed from their skewers) and serve.

NOTES AND TIPS

✦ *You can also serve your koftas on a plate with the sauce, salad and pitta separately.*

✦ *Any time you have stale bread, process or blend it into a batch of breadcrumbs and freeze in small bags. They will thaw in a minute in a microwave.*

Thai Pork with Almonds

SERVES 2

CALORIES PER PORTION: 330	PROTEIN: HIGH
TOTAL FAT PER PORTION: 18g	CARBOHYDRATE: ★
SATURATED FAT PER PORTION: 3g	FIBRE: ★★

A clean-tasting little stir-fry to knock together in minutes – much, much quicker, definitely less fattening, and probably nicer than going to the local Thai take-away.

250g (9 oz) pork tenderloin	I tablespoon dry to medium sherry
I tablespoon sesame oil	I tablespoon soy sauce
8 spring onions, trimmed and halved lengthways	25g (I oz) toasted flaked almonds
I large or 2 small courgettes, cut into thin strips or ribbons	50ml (2 fl oz) chicken stock mixed with I teaspoon cornflour
I teaspoon Thai seven-spice seasoning	

Cut the tenderloin into 1 cm (½ inch) slices, then cut each slice into two. Heat the oil in a wok or large non-stick frying pan and, when really hot, add the pork and stir-fry for 2 minutes until tinged golden. Add the vegetables and stir-fry for 2 minutes more on high. Turn the heat down slightly and add the seasoning, sherry and soy sauce, and stir for another 2 minutes. Toss in the almonds and stir for 1 minute, then add the stock and cornflour mixture, stir and bubble for 1 minute. Serve immediately.

NOTES AND TIPS
✦ *You could use chicken instead of pork.*
✦ *Serve with egg thread noodles or boiled rice.*

Mildly Spiced Pork Brochettes with a Mango and Lime Sauce

SERVES 2

CALORIES PER PORTION: 296	PROTEIN: HIGH
TOTAL FAT PER PORTION: 10g	CARBOHYDRATE: ★
SATURATED FAT PER PORTION: 4g	FIBRE: ★

THIS is one of my very favourite ways to cook pork. It has all the lovely flavours of a mild korma curry – without the effort and without the calories!

300 g (11 oz) pork tenderloin	2 tablespoons mango chutney
125 ml (4½ fl oz) half-fat Greek yogurt	juice of 1 lime
½ teaspoon each of mustard powder, and ground cumin, coriander and ginger	1 tablespoon chopped fresh coriander

Preheat the grill. Cut the pork into 2 cm (³/₄ inch) cubes and put in a bowl. Mix the yogurt with the spices, and then mix this into the pork pieces to coat thoroughly. Thread the pork pieces on to two skewers (if bamboo, pre-soak for 30 minutes in water). Grill the brochettes for 10 minutes, turning regularly and basting with leftover marinade for the first few minutes. Mix together the chutney, lime juice and coriander, and serve with the brochettes.

NOTES AND TIPS

✦ *If you plan ahead, or have time, leave the pork pieces in the spiced yogurt marinade for an hour or more (up to 8 hours) in the fridge.*

✦ *If you can get your hands on a fresh, ripe mango, you could make the sauce with this, finely chopping it and adding the lime juice and coriander with just a dash of mango chutney to sweeten.*

✦ *Serve with wild and basmati rice at 20 calories a tablespoon (cooked).*

Pork Stroganoff

<u>SERVES 2</u>

CALORIES PER PORTION: 305	PROTEIN: HIGH
TOTAL FAT PER PORTION: 18g	CARBOHYDRATE: ★
SATURATED FAT PER PORTION: 7g	FIBRE: ★★

A quick and luxurious dish that is as suitable for a supper party as for a TV dinner. Served with plenty of noodles or rice and a big green salad, it also makes a nutritionally well-balanced meal.

200 g (7 oz) pork tenderloin	50 ml (2 fl oz) chicken stock
1 tablespoon corn or groundnut (peanut) oil	100 ml (3½ fl oz) low-fat crème fraîche
1 medium onion, finely chopped	1 teaspoon Hungarian paprika, plus extra to serve
1 tablespoon brandy (optional)	salt and freshly ground black pepper
125 g (4½ oz) small mushrooms	

Cut the pork tenderloin into 1 cm (½ inch) slices, then halve each slice. Pat the pork pieces dry on absorbent kitchen paper if necessary. Heat the oil in a non-stick frying pan until very hot. Add the pork and leave for 1–2 minutes until the underside of each piece is sealed and golden. (If you stir the pork around before this it might stick.) Turn the pieces and brown the other side, then remove to a warm plate for a minute using a slotted spatula.

Add the onion to the pan and stir-fry on a slightly lower heat for about 8 minutes or until soft and just turning golden. Return the meat to the pan and stir-fry for another minute, then add the brandy, if using, and, when bubbling, add the mushrooms and stock, turn the heat down and simmer for 2 minutes. Add the crème fraîche, paprika and seasoning, stir and let everything barely simmer for a further 2 minutes. Check the seasoning and serve dusted with paprika.

NOTES AND TIPS

✦ *This recipe also works well with lean beef or well-hung venison.*

OPPOSITE: Pork Stroganoff (above)

OPPOSITE PAGE 43: Chicken with Two Cheeses and Ham (page 53)

Bacon, Potato and Broccoli Gratin

<u>SERVES 2</u>

CALORIES PER PORTION: 328	PROTEIN: HIGH
TOTAL FAT PER PORTION: 12g	CARBOHYDRATE: ★★
SATURATED FAT PER PORTION: 3.5g	FIBRE: ★★

THIS is a knockout treat for the tastebuds – a homely, warming supper which proves perfectly that there *is* such a thing as comfort food even when you are trying to lose weight!

400 g (14 oz) new potatoes, scraped or lightly peeled	125 g (4½ oz) broccoli, broken into small florets
1 tablespoon olive oil	50 g (2 oz) firm mushrooms, sliced
1 medium red onion, cut into smallish chunks	salt and freshly ground black pepper
3 extra-lean back bacon rashers (about 75 g/3 oz total weight)	40 g (1½ oz) grated half-fat Mozzarella cheese (see note)

Cut the potatoes in half (or quarters if they are the size of an egg or bigger) and cook them in lightly salted boiling water for 15 minutes or until tender. Meanwhile, heat the oil in a flameproof gratin dish, add the onion, and cook over a medium heat, stirring occasionally.

Remove every last trace of fat from the bacon, if necessary, and cut into strips. Add to the gratin dish, stir and continue cooking, turning the heat up a little, until the onion is soft and golden and the bacon crisp. This should take about 10 minutes from the time you added the onion. Preheat the grill.

Pop the broccoli in with the potatoes to cook for the last 3 minutes of their cooking time. Meanwhile, add the mushrooms to the gratin dish and stir for 1 minute. Carefully remove the broccoli from the top of the potatoes with a slotted spoon, and set aside. Drain the potatoes well and stir into the onion mixture thoroughly. Dot the broccoli pieces around the dish, season with plenty of pepper and a very little salt, and top with the cheese, distributing it evenly over the dish. Flash the gratin under the grill for about 2 minutes or until the cheese has melted and the gratin is turning golden. Eat immediately!

NOTES AND TIPS
✦ *You could use halved cherry tomatoes instead of the mushrooms, or even par-boiled green beans or very thinly sliced leeks.*
✦ *You can buy ready-grated half-fat Mozzarella in most supermarkets.*

Italian Meatballs in Tomato Sauce

<u>SERVES 2</u>

CALORIES PER PORTION: 317	PROTEIN: HIGH
TOTAL FAT PER PORTION: 11 g	CARBOHYDRATE: ★
SATURATED FAT PER PORTION: 3 g	FIBRE: ★★

MEATBALLS are enjoying a comeback in all the best kitchens, and provide a welcome opportunity to use mince for something other than spag bol, cottage pie or lasagne! I think they are lovely – in a rich tomato sauce and served with rice or tagliatelle, they make a meal fit for any Italian count or bored slimmer.

200 g (7 oz) extra-lean finely minced organic beef or lamb fillet or pork	salt and freshly ground black pepper
	1 tablespoon olive oil
25 g (1 oz) dry breadcrumbs	1 clove garlic, finely chopped
1 medium to large Spanish onion, very finely chopped	200 g (7 oz) can chopped tomatoes with basil
	100 ml (3½ fl oz) passata
1 tablespoon finely chopped fresh parsley	pinch of sugar
pinch of ground cinnamon	2 teaspoons tomato purée
1 egg white	1 teaspoon lemon juice

In a bowl, mix together the first seven ingredients, reserving a good half of the onion. Heat the oil in a large non-stick pan and, while it is heating, divide the meat mixture into twelve small balls, using your hands. Add the meatballs to the pan and brown on all sides over a high heat. Turn the heat down and add the remaining ingredients to the pan, including the reserved onion. Stir well, bring to a simmer, cover and simmer very gently for 20 minutes or until you have a rich sauce. Check the seasoning before serving.

NOTES AND TIPS
✦ *If you have any fresh basil leaves to hand, toss some on to the dish to serve.*
✦ *Adjust the amount of passata you add to the sauce to taste. You might need a little less or a little more than the 100 ml (3½ fl oz).*
✦ *The meatballs are also very nice served with a pile of couscous or bulghar wheat.*

Venison Steaks in Red Wine

SERVES 2

CALORIES PER PORTION: 293	PROTEIN: HIGH
TOTAL FAT PER PORTION: 8g	CARBOHYDRATE: ★
SATURATED FAT PER PORTION: 2g	FIBRE: ★

I don't think we can sensibly call venison 'game' any more, as nearly all of what we eat is farmed, just like pigs or sheep or, indeed, ostrich, now is. It also tastes very meaty and, as it is so low in fat, is an excellent substitute for beef in almost any beef recipe. Try to make sure, though, that for quick-cook recipes, you buy venison that has been well hung, otherwise it might be tough.

two 150g (5½oz) venison steaks	2 teaspoons plain flour
125ml (4½fl oz) red wine	salt and freshly ground black pepper
I tablespoon olive oil	I tablespoon finely chopped fresh tarragon or
150g (5oz) shallots, finely chopped	parsley
pinch of sugar	

If you plan ahead or have time, leave the venison steaks to marinate in the red wine in a shallow bowl for up to 8 hours. Otherwise, proceed as follows: heat the oil in a non-stick frying pan and stir-fry the shallots over a medium-high heat for 2–3 minutes until soft. Add the venison steaks and, keeping the heat high, leave them alone for 3–4 minutes (depending on thickness) until well browned on the underside. Turn the steaks over and brown the other side, giving the onions a stir as you do so and adding the sugar.

Remove the steaks from the pan and keep warm. Add the flour to the pan with a little salt and plenty of freshly ground black pepper. Stir for 1 minute, adding a little of the wine if the mix seems too dry. Add the rest of the wine and the herbs, heat until bubbling, then allow to simmer for 2 minutes. Serve the steaks with the sauce.

NOTES AND TIPS
✦ *You can use lean fillet or rump organic beef in this recipe instead, which will slightly increase the calorie and fat contents.*
✦ *Serve with new potatoes and plenty of spinach or spring greens.*

Venison in Cider Apple Sauce

SERVES 2

CALORIES PER PORTION: 320	PROTEIN: HIGH
TOTAL FAT PER PORTION: 14g	CARBOHYDRATE: ★
SATURATED FAT PER PORTION: 6.5g	FIBRE: ★

CIDER is more commonly used when cooking pork or chicken, but it works surprisingly well with venison. Be sure to use good-quality venison steak in this recipe, rather than the stewing cuts, which need slow casseroling to become tender.

15g (½oz) butter	1 mild onion *or* 4 large shallots, very finely chopped
2 teaspoons corn oil	1 eating apple
two 150g (5½oz) venison steaks, cut into bite-sized cubes	50ml (2fl oz) dry cider
	1 tablespoon half-fat crème fraîche
salt and freshly ground black pepper	

Heat the butter and oil in a heavy-based non-stick frying pan and, when sizzling, add the pieces of venison, spreading them evenly around the pan and seasoning with salt and pepper. Leave over high heat for 2 minutes to brown (if you move them around they might stick), then turn them over and brown for a further 2 minutes. Turn the heat down to medium and remove the meat from the pan with a slotted spoon. Add the onion or shallots to the pan and cook for a few minutes until soft. While the onion is cooking, core the apple and chop into 1 cm (½inch) pieces. Add to the pan and cook for about 2 minutes or until turning golden. Add the cider and stir, then return the meat, and any juices that have run out, to the pan, and allow to simmer for 2 minutes. Finally, stir in the crème fraîche, check the seasoning and serve.

NOTES AND TIPS
✦ *Serve with mashed potatoes and green vegetables.*

Venison Sausage and Bean Supper

<u>Serves 2</u>

CALORIES PER PORTION: 278	PROTEIN: HIGH
TOTAL FAT PER PORTION: 6 g	CARBOHYDRATE: ★★
SATURATED FAT PER PORTION: 1.5 g	FIBRE: ★★★

VENISON sausages make a welcome alternative to beef or pork and I think they are tastier. They are also lower in saturated fat. Here they combine well with borlotti beans in a robust, high-fibre supper for a cold evening.

Fry Light cooking spray (see page 4)	2 medium sticks celery, very thinly sliced
3 large venison sausages (about 150 g/5½ oz total weight)	200 g (7 oz) can chopped tomatoes with herbs
	200 g (7 oz) can borlotti beans, drained
1 medium Spanish onion, finely chopped	1 tablespoon sun-dried tomato purée
1 clove garlic, chopped	1 tablespoon chopped fresh basil or marjoram
1 large carrot, very thinly sliced	salt and freshly ground black pepper

Heat a sauté pan or flameproof casserole sprayed with Fry Light. Cut the sausages into four chunks each and add to the pan as it heats up so that the sausages begin to cook in their own fat. Gradually turn the heat up so that the sausages brown. After 3–4 minutes, add the onion and garlic and stir for 1 minute, then add the carrot and celery and allow to cook, stirring from time to time, for 3 minutes more. Add the tomatoes, beans, tomato purée, herbs and seasoning, stir well, bring to a simmer and simmer, covered, for 20 minutes or until everything is tender. Check the seasoning and serve.

NOTES AND TIPS
✦ *You could use a different variety of canned beans in this supper if you like – butter beans, lima beans, or a mixed can would all be nice.*
✦ *If the casserole seems a bit dry at any stage, add a little water or passata to the pan, stirring in well.*

Beef and Pepper Stir-fry

<u>SERVES 2</u>

CALORIES PER PORTION: 267	PROTEIN: HIGH
TOTAL FAT PER PORTION: 11 g	CARBOHYDRATE: ★
SATURATED FAT PER PORTION: 3 g	FIBRE: ★★

PORK, lamb and turkey also work well in this recipe – indeed, you could even use tofu or Quorn chunks.

1 tablespoon sesame oil	100 g (3½ oz) fresh beansprouts
225 g (8 oz) extra-lean rump or fillet steak, cut into thin strips	1 tablespoon light soy sauce
	2 tablespoons black bean sauce (see note)
2 small to medium red peppers, de-seeded and cut into thin strips	4 tablespoons beef or other stock mixed with 1 teaspoon cornflour
8 spring onions, trimmed and halved lengthways	

Heat the oil in a wok or non-stick frying pan and, when very hot, add the meat and stir-fry for 1 minute until well sealed and brown. Add the peppers, and stir on a slightly lower heat for another 3 minutes. Add the onions, beansprouts, soy sauce and a very little water, and stir-fry again for a further 2 minutes. Add the black bean sauce and stir, then pour in the stock and cornflour mixture and stir until the sauce has thickened.

NOTES AND TIPS
✦ *This is nice with either rice, medium egg noodles or rice noodles.*
✦ *Black bean sauce comes in jars and is widely available.*
✦ *You can add other vegetables if you like – green beans, carrots, mushrooms – all cut into thin pieces. Add them with the peppers and increase the cooking time a little.*

CHAPTER FIVE

POULTRY AND GAME

Chicken and turkey (with the skin removed) are well known now as ideal fare for slimmers, but endless poultry meals can get a little boring. The recipes in this chapter will help you to think of new ways of cooking them.

Game meats can also be perfect as part of a slimming plan – but not all game meats are low in calories and fat. Duck – the ordinary, Norfolk type – is an extremely high-fat bird and even when it is roasted until almost all the fat seems to have melted into the pan, it still contains a great deal of fat. A much better choice is the Barbary duck, which is meatier and less fatty. Or, even better, a small wild duck, which has plenty of exquisitely flavoured meaty flesh and precious little fat at all. Other excellent types of game are rabbit, low in both fat and calories, and all the 'new' meats, such as crocodile, kangaroo, boar, buffalo and ostrich. Grouse, pheasant, pigeon and partridge are four more tasty, low-fat birds. The choice is now so wide, it is a pity to rely too heavily on chicken. If you do choose chicken, I suggest you buy either corn-fed or free-range birds, which have more flavour than their poor battery-reared cousins.

Here are a few ideas for cheering up chicken if you've only a minute or two to spare:

★ Many herbs go excellently with chicken – sprinkle chopped tarragon and/or rosemary and thyme or basil on to sliced chicken breasts, and dry-fry in Fry Light (see page 4), adding a dash of white wine towards the end of the cooking time.

★ Brush chicken portions with olive oil and sprinkle on some ready-made barbecue seasoning (powdered form) before barbecuing or grilling.

★ Cut a slit in chicken breast portions and fill the slit with crushed garlic, a pinch of garam marsala and some chopped dried apricots before poaching in a very little stock.

Chicken and Mushrooms in Cider Sauce

<u>SERVES 2</u>

CALORIES PER PORTION: 283	PROTEIN: HIGH
TOTAL FAT PER PORTION: 10g	CARBOHYDRATE: ★
SATURATED FAT PER PORTION: 2.5 G	FIBRE: ★

THIS rich-sounding dish is tasty but actually quite light. And it is extremely easy to cook.

10g (¼oz) dried mushrooms, e.g. *porcini*	50–75 ml (2–3 fl oz) dry cider
1 tablespoon corn oil	2 sprigs fresh thyme
2 medium chicken breast fillets, skinned and each sliced in two	freshly ground black pepper
	100g (3½oz) Shape low-fat soft cheese
100g (3½oz) small chestnut mushrooms, sliced	a little skimmed milk
2 spring onions, very finely chopped	

Put the dried mushrooms in a bowl, cover with a little hot water and leave to soak. Heat the oil in a non-stick pan and cook the chicken pieces over a high heat until sealed and golden. Add the chestnut mushrooms and stir for 1–2 minutes or until they too are golden. Drain the dried mushrooms and add to the pan with the spring onions. Stir again for 1 minute. Stir in most of the cider, turn the heat down to medium low, add the thyme and season with pepper, and let the dish simmer for 5 minutes or until the chicken is tender. Tip in the cheese, which will slowly melt. Add a little skimmed milk to the pan when the cheese has melted, along with a dash of the remaining cider (or all of the remaining cider if the sauce seems a little too dry), stir and serve.

NOTES AND TIPS
✦ *Serve with new potatoes or pasta.*

Spicy Skewered Chicken

SERVES 2

CALORIES PER PORTION: 186	PROTEIN: HIGH
TOTAL FAT PER PORTION: 3 g	CARBOHYDRATE: ★
SATURATED FAT PER PORTION: 1 g	FIBRE: ★

A very simple way of spicing up chicken thighs for a tasty supper based on storecupboard ingredients. Serve with plenty of salad and some rice for a complete meal.

4 skinned and boned chicken thighs	1 teaspoon soy sauce
1 rounded tablespoon tomato purée	2 teaspoons dried rosemary
1 tablespoon runny honey	8 cherry tomatoes
1 tablespoon Worcestershire sauce	

Preheat the grill. Cut the chicken into bite-sized cubes. In a shallow bowl, mix together the tomato purée, honey, Worcestershire sauce, soy sauce and rosemary, add the chicken cubes and stir to coat well. (If you have time or have planned ahead, at this stage you could leave the chicken to marinate for up to 8 hours; even 30 minutes would do.) Thread the chicken and tomatoes on to four small or two large kebab skewers or sticks (see note) and grill for 8–10 minutes, turning once and basting with any surplus sauce.

NOTES AND TIPS
+ *Try to find kebab skewers with angular surfaces, rather than the smooth, round ones. The bits of meat, veg, and so on, tend to have an annoying habit of doing cartwheels on those round skewers, so as fast as you try to turn them, they end up back where they started. Wooden (or bamboo) sticks are good, too, but you need to pre-soak them to prevent them burning.*
+ *Some cooking foil underneath the kebabs on the grill pan will help you save the marinade sauce and produce a more succulent result, as well as keeping the grill pan clean.*

Tarragon Chicken

<u>SERVES 2</u>

CALORIES PER PORTION: 303	PROTEIN: HIGH
TOTAL FAT PER PORTION: 14.5 g	CARBOHYDRATE: ★
SATURATED FAT PER PORTION: 7 g	FIBRE: ★

YOU can find fresh tarragon now in many supermarkets, and it is easy to grow yourself from seed, or you can buy a small plant at a garden centre. A little goes a long way so one plant would be enough. Dried tarragon is nowhere near so good.

2 teaspoons butter	3 tablespoons light chicken stock
2 teaspoons corn oil	50 ml (2 fl oz) half-fat single cream
2 skinned chicken breast fillets (about 300 g/11 oz total weight)	50 ml (2 fl oz) 8% fat fromage frais
	1 tablespoon chopped fresh tarragon
3 tablespoons dry white wine	a little salt if necessary
freshly ground black pepper	4 sprigs fresh tarragon to garnish

Heat the butter and oil in a non-stick frying pan. While it is heating, cut each chicken breast into two or three pieces. Add the chicken to the pan and leave for 2 minutes without stirring until the undersides are golden. Turn and repeat. Add the wine, season with pepper, and allow to bubble for a few seconds. Add the stock, turn down the heat, cover the pan and allow to simmer for 5–6 minutes or until the chicken is cooked and tender.

Meanwhile, mix together the half-fat cream and the fromage frais, and add the chopped tarragon to this mixture, stirring. When the chicken is ready, spoon the cream mixture into the pan and heat through. Check the seasoning, adding salt if necessary, and serve garnished with tarragon sprigs.

NOTES AND TIPS
✦ *This dish is nice served with new potatoes, green beans and broccoli.*

Chicken with Two Cheeses and Ham

<u>SERVES 2</u>

CALORIES PER PORTION: 280
TOTAL FAT PER PORTION: 9.5 g
SATURATED FAT PER PORTION: 3.5 g

PROTEIN: HIGH
CARBOHYDRATE: ★
FIBRE: ★

ONE of my favourite suppers is lean chicken pieces wrapped in lean bacon and baked in the oven with garlic, white wine and various seasonings. But I couldn't make that work in 30 minutes, so here is a similar dish that you can create within that time and with a delicate, creamy result. People should poach chicken more often!

2 skinned chicken fillets (about 300 g/11 oz total weight)

chicken stock

50 g (2 oz) low-fat soft cheese, e.g. Tartare Light or Boursin Light

2 slices extra-lean smoked ham

2 tablespoons ready-grated half-fat Mozzarella cheese

Place the chicken breasts in a small saucepan and add enough chicken stock to cover. Poach the breasts (so that the stock barely simmers) for 15 minutes or until cooked through and tender. Keep checking and making sure that the stock isn't bubbling too hard. Preheat the grill. Remove the chicken from the stock and spread the cheese on top of each breast, then cover with a slice of ham. Finish with the grated cheese. Flash under the grill until the cheese bubbles and starts to turn golden.

NOTES AND TIPS

✦ *If you have a microwave you could poach the chicken in a couple of tablespoons of stock on medium for 5 minutes (check your oven's instructions for an exact time and wattage).*

✦ *This dish would go well with a basil and tomato salad and some new potatoes.*

✦ *You could also make this dish using turkey fillets instead of chicken.*

Chicken and Avocado Enchiladas

<u>SERVES 2</u>

CALORIES PER PORTION: 509	PROTEIN: HIGH
TOTAL FAT PER PORTION: 18 g	CARBOHYDRATE: ★
SATURATED FAT PER PORTION: 3 g	FIBRE: ★★★

MEXICAN food offers masses of flavour, colour and mouth satisfaction. Some Mexican dishes can be high in fat, but most traditional recipes can be adapted to bring them well within your range, as I've done with this one.

Fry Light cooking spray (see page 4)

250 g (9 oz) breast of chicken (no skin), diced

2 teaspoons corn oil

1 teaspoon crushed chilli flakes

1 medium red and 1 medium yellow pepper,
 de-seeded and sliced

1 medium red onion, sliced

200 g (7 oz) chopped tomatoes

1 small avocado

2 generous tablespoons 0% fat fromage frais

1 teaspoon lemon juice

1 teaspoon Tabasco (hot pepper) sauce

2 ready-made flour tortillas

To garnish

crisp lettuce, shredded

fresh coriander leaves

2 tablespoons natural low-fat Bio yogurt

Heat a large non-stick frying pan sprayed with Fry Light. While it is heating, toss the chicken pieces with the oil and chilli flakes. Add them to the pan and allow to sizzle for 2–3 minutes. Add the peppers and onion, stir for a few minutes over a high heat, and then turn the heat down and add the tomatoes. Allow to simmer for a few minutes or until the vegetables have lost much of their 'bite' but are still firm. Meanwhile, halve and stone the avocado, peel it, and chop it into a bowl. Add the fromage frais, lemon juice and Tabasco, and mix well.

When the chicken mixture is nearly ready, heat the tortillas under a moderately hot grill for a minute to warm through, and cut each into quarters. Serve the chicken in two bowls with the tortillas around the edge, and the avocado mixture piled on top. Garnish with lettuce, coriander leaves and 1 tablespoon yogurt.

NOTES AND TIPS
✦ *Ready-made tortillas are available in the Mexican sections of large supermarkets.*
✦ *Add extra chilli flakes and/or Tabasco if you prefer a hotter taste.*

Chicken Satay with Peanut Sauce

<u>SERVES 2</u>

CALORIES PER PORTION: 306	PROTEIN: HIGH
TOTAL FAT PER PORTION: 14 g	CARBOHYDRATE: ★
SATURATED FAT PER PORTION: 3 g	FIBRE: ★

CHICKEN satay is almost always regarded as a 'no-no' for slimmers and weight-watchers, but with a little bit of cunning you can reduce the fat content of the peanut sauce quite considerably and make it into a dish suitable, if not for every other day, then at least for once in a while!

300 g (11 oz) skinned and boned chicken breast	2 tablespoons chunky peanut butter
juice of 1–2 limes	2 tablespoons 0% fat fromage frais
2 teaspoons light soy sauce	dash of Tabasco (hot pepper) sauce
2 teaspoons groundnut (peanut) oil	a little skimmed milk
½ teaspoon chilli flakes	salt and freshly ground black pepper

Preheat the grill. Cut the chicken into bite-sized pieces and thread on to pre-soaked bamboo satay sticks or metal kebab skewers. Place on foil on the grill pan, and brush on half the lime juice, then the soy sauce, then the oil, then sprinkle on the chilli flakes. (If at this stage you have time to leave the chicken to marinate for 30 minutes or so, so much the better.)

Grill the chicken for 3–4 minutes on one side, then 3 minutes on the other, basting with any sauce that runs off on to the foil. Meanwhile, make the sauce by beating together the peanut butter, fromage frais, Tabasco, remaining lime juice and enough skimmed milk to give it a consistency between a dip and a sauce. Check the seasoning and, when the chicken is golden and ready, serve it with the sauce.

NOTES AND TIPS

✦ *You can warm the sauce if you like, very gently, in a microwave or tiny saucepan.*
✦ *You could make this dish using pork tenderloin pieces instead for roughly the same calorie and fat counts.*
✦ *Serve with rice or some wholemeal pitta bread.*

Turkey and Apple Burgers

SERVES 2

CALORIES PER PORTION: 380	PROTEIN: HIGH
TOTAL FAT PER PORTION: 11 g	CARBOHYDRATE: ★★
SATURATED FAT PER PORTION: 2 g	FIBRE: ★★

WHEN cooking my Christmas turkey, I put plenty of chopped apple in the chestnut stuffing, and these turkey and apple burgers work on the same principle – the apple gives the burgers succulence as well as an appealing tang.

150 g (5½ oz) turkey mince	salt and freshly ground black pepper
1 shallot, finely chopped	1 small egg, beaten
1 small cooking apple, peeled, cored and finely chopped	Fry Light cooking spray (see page 4)
	2 rings cut from a cored eating apple
25 g (1 oz) dry breadcrumbs	2 wholemeal baps
2 teaspoons chopped mixed nuts	2 teaspoons mango chutney

In a bowl, mix together the turkey mince, shallot, apple, breadcrumbs, nuts and seasoning, then mix in the beaten egg to bind. Form into two large, round patties about 1 cm (½ inch) thick. Heat a non-stick frying pan sprayed with Fry Light and, when really hot, add the burgers. Cook for 5 minutes on one side, then turn and cook on the other side. Add the apple rings to the pan for the last few minutes of cooking, pressing them down with a spatula so that they soften, and turn slightly golden. When the burgers are thoroughly cooked, serve them in the baps, garnished with the apple slices and chutney.

NOTES AND TIPS
✦ *Serve with a large salad.*

Turkey and Cashew Nut Stir-fry

<u>SERVES 2</u>

CALORIES PER PORTION: 310	PROTEIN: HIGH
TOTAL FAT PER PORTION: 14g	CARBOHYDRATE: ★
SATURATED FAT PER PORTION: 3g	FIBRE: ★★

TURKEY makes one of *the* best stir-fries – stronger tasting than chicken, it marries well with the robust flavours characteristic of stir-frying. It is also very low in fat, quick to cook – and comes ready-prepared in handy stir-fry packs at the supermarket.

200g (7oz) pack turkey prepared for stir-frying	6 spring onions, trimmed and halved lengthways
2 tablespoons soy sauce	I small red chilli, de-seeded and chopped (see note)
I tablespoon sesame oil	I tablespoon oyster sauce (see note)
25g (I oz) unsalted cashew nuts	I teaspoon runny honey
75g (3oz) green beans, cut in half	I tablespoon medium or dry sherry (optional)
75g (3oz) carrots, cut into thin strips	2–3 tablespoons chicken stock mixed with
25g (I oz) baby sweetcorn	I teaspoon cornflour

If necessary, cut the turkey into thin, even strips. Sprinkle over 1 tablespoon of the soy sauce. (If at this stage you can leave it to marinate, so much the better, otherwise continue with the recipe.) Heat the oil in a wok or large non-stick frying pan and, when very hot, add the turkey pieces and stir-fry for 2 minutes to brown. For the last half minute, add the nuts.

Remove the turkey and nuts from the pan and add all the vegetables. Stir-fry for 3 minutes over a high heat. Add the remaining soy sauce, chilli, oyster sauce, honey and sherry, and return the turkey and nuts to the pan. Stir-fry for 3 minutes, adding a little water or chicken stock (not the cornflour mix) if the stir-fry looks too dry. When the turkey is cooked, add the stock and cornflour mix, stirring well until thickened. Serve straight away.

NOTES AND TIPS
✦ *Oyster sauce is a rich and delicious sauce which you can buy, bottled, in the supermarket. It isn't really fishy, it just adds marvellous flavour to stir-fries.*
✦ *If you haven't got fresh chilli, use 1 teaspoon chilli flakes.*
✦ *Serve the stir-fry with medium egg noodles or rice.*

Breast of Pheasant with Leek and Mushrooms

SERVES 2

CALORIES PER PORTION: 318	PROTEIN: HIGH
TOTAL FAT PER PORTION: 20g	CARBOHYDRATE: ★
SATURATED FAT PER PORTION: 6g	FIBRE: ★

PHEASANT is a tender, low-fat bird with a delicious flavour a little like an extremely tasty chicken. Or at least, it should be. If it isn't hung long enough it can be tough; if it is hung too long, it can taste too strong for some people's liking. Don't let me put you off, though – just buy from someone you trust. See also the notes at the end of the recipe on picking a good bird.

1 tablespoon olive or corn oil	1 clove garlic, crushed
2 breasts of pheasant (see note)	2 tablespoons dry white wine (see note)
2 teaspoons chopped fresh sage or 1 teaspoon dried	2 tablespoons chicken stock
100 g (3½ oz) small chestnut mushrooms, sliced	1 tablespoon half-fat crème fraîche
1 leek or 1 stick celery, thinly sliced	sage leaves to garnish

Heat the oil in a sauté pan with a lid, add the pheasant and brown over a high heat for 2 minutes. Turn the heat down, add the chopped or dried sage, mushrooms, leek or celery and garlic, and stir for 1 minute. Add the wine and stock, bubble, cover and simmer over a low heat for 15 minutes or until the pheasant breasts are cooked and tender. Remove the pheasant to a serving plate and keep warm. Add the crème fraîche to the pan and stir into the sauce. Serve with the pheasant, garnished with sage leaves.

NOTES AND TIPS

✦ *Male pheasants are bigger than female pheasants and often slightly less tender. Ask what sex the bird is and plump for a female if you can. If the bird isn't packaged, give it a sniff, too; if it smells very strong, it will probably taste very strong, but if it has no smell at all it may not have been hung long enough. Some shops sell pheasant breasts but if you buy a whole pheasant, joint it yourself and freeze the legs which will make a nice addition to a casserole.*

✦ *This recipe also works well with rabbit fillets or guinea fowl.*

✦ *If preferred, omit the wine and double the amount of stock used.*

Rabbit with Herbes de Provence

<u>SERVES 2</u>

CALORIES PER PORTION: 378
TOTAL FAT PER PORTION: 15.5g
SATURATED FAT PER PORTION: 4.5g

PROTEIN: HIGH
CARBOHYDRATE: ★
FIBRE: ★★

RABBIT is neglected in the UK, which is a shame as it is very low in fat and has a lovely delicate flavour. See if you can find some rabbit fillets and give this recipe a go.

1 tablespoon olive oil	50 ml (2 fl oz) dry white wine
fillets from one rabbit (see note)	50 ml (2 fl oz) chicken stock (see note)
1 small onion, finely chopped	1 clove garlic, crushed
2 teaspoons each chopped fresh fennel, thyme, rosemary and marjoram or 1 teaspoon each dried or 2 teaspoons Herbes de Provence	1 rounded teaspoon plain flour
	salt and freshly ground black pepper
	fresh herbs to garnish
4 stoned ready-to-eat prunes, finely chopped (see note)	

Heat the oil in a non-stick, lidded sauté pan and brown the rabbit pieces for 1 minute over a high heat. Add the onion and stir-fry for 2 minutes to soften. Add the herbs, prunes, wine, stock and garlic, sprinkle the flour over, and stir to combine. Season, cover and simmer for 20 minutes or until the rabbit is tender, stirring halfway through. Check the seasoning and serve with a herb garnish.

NOTES AND TIPS
✦ *You can use all stock instead of the wine and stock, if you like.*
✦ *Your game merchant should be able to fillet the rabbit for you – use only the back fillet and legs.*
✦ *Don't be put off by the idea of using prunes in a savoury dish. They add a wonderful fruity succulence to the rabbit and to the sauce.*
✦ *If you have more time, you can use rabbit pieces on the bone, which will take longer to cook (about 1 hour).*

Duck with Orange and Ginger

<u>SERVES 2</u>

CALORIES PER PORTION: 326
TOTAL FAT PER PORTION: 15 g
SATURATED FAT PER PORTION: 4 g

PROTEIN: HIGH
CARBOHYDRATE: ★
FIBRE: ★★

PEOPLE tend to think of duck as a fatty food, but a breast fillet with the skin, and all visible fat underneath the skin, removed, is no more fatty than any other lean meat. Choose a meaty Barbary duck for this recipe – the flavour is superb and the meat lovely and tender.

2 breasts of Barbary duck, skin removed (about 200 g/7 oz after skinning)	2 cm (¾ inch) knob fresh root ginger, peeled and chopped
1 tablespoon groundnut (peanut) oil	1 tablespoon light soy sauce
1 small red onion, very thinly sliced	grated rind of ½ orange
1 clove garlic, chopped	2 tablespoons orange juice
75 g (3 oz) broccoli, cut into tiny florets	2 teaspoons plum sauce (see note)
100 g (3½ oz) sweet potato (orange-fleshed kind) or butternut squash, peeled and cut into thin batons (see note)	2 tablespoons chicken or lamb stock mixed with ½ teaspoon cornflour
50 g (2 oz) mangetout	2 teaspoons toasted sesame seeds

Cut each duck breast diagonally into five (or so) slices, and then cut each slice into two. Heat the oil in a wok or non-stick frying pan and, when sizzling, add the duck and brown on all sides for 1–2 minutes. Add the onion, garlic, broccoli and sweet potato or squash and stir-fry for 3 minutes, turning the heat down slightly after 1 minute. Add the mangetout, ginger, soy sauce, orange rind and orange juice, and stir for another 2 minutes. Finally, add the plum sauce and stock and cornflour mix, stirring well. Allow to bubble and thicken, then serve garnished with sesame seeds.

NOTES AND TIPS
✦ *Use bottled plum sauce, available at most supermarkets – it will be in the 'ethnic' section – and delicatessens.*
✦ *If you can't get sweet potato or squash, you can use carrots instead.*

CHAPTER SIX

FISH AND SHELLFISH

S adly, very many people I know rarely eat fish. When I ask why, most of them say that they find fish boring, it doesn't satisfy hunger or, even worse, it contains bones! Luckily, chefs such as Rick Stein and Keith Floyd are slowly changing our opinion of fish, and I would like to add my small voice here because, for slimmers especially, fish can be a wonderful regular addition to the diet.

Ten or twenty years ago, the choice of fish in our shops was very limited and what was available was often not as fresh as it could be. If you didn't fancy cod, haddock or plaice, that was it. But now, well, the list is almost endless. It seems that nearly every week I spot a new fish variety in the shops, and there is certainly no longer any shortage of excellent fish recipes to try.

Admittedly, a small fillet of plaice or lemon sole isn't much of a hunger-stopper, but again, these days there are so many robust, meaty-types of fish to be found that this old excuse no longer holds good. In this chapter I've made full use of these gutsy fish – tuna, swordfish, shark, skate, salmon and many more are ideal for people who 'don't like fish'. You will also, by the way, find the original filling fish dish, real fish and chips, in this chapter – a good, old-fashioned meal surprisingly low in calories and fat.

Lastly – the answer to bones: buy filleted fish, or fish such as skate and swordfish which don't have tiny bones to annoy you.

All white fish and shellfish are low in calories and fat. Oily fish, such as mackerel, herring and salmon, are higher in fat and therefore calories, but you should still eat them because they contain special fats called omega-3s which offer protection from heart and circulatory disease when eaten regularly.

When you're looking for something quick to do with fish, turn to the spicy flavours of the East – try lime juice, chilli, coriander, lemon grass, soy sauce, ginger. A stir-fry using any combination of these flavours with fish will always turn out wonderfully.

Swordfish with Tomato Salsa

<u>SERVES 2</u>

CALORIES PER PORTION: 280   PROTEIN: HIGH
TOTAL FAT PER PORTION: 13 g   CARBOHYDRATE: ★
SATURATED FAT PER PORTION: 3 g   FIBRE: ★

ANY succulent, firm white fish can be used in this recipe. I particularly like the robustness of swordfish, but the more delicate taste of cod is very good, and the gutsy tuna steak is another alternative, although it will be a little higher in calories because it contains more of the 'good for you' omega-3 oils.

2 swordfish steaks (about 200 g/7 oz each)	4 pitted black olives
2 teaspoons olive oil	1 very small red onion
salt and freshly ground black pepper	2 teaspoons chopped fresh coriander or flat-leaved
juice of 2 limes	parsley
2 tasty tomatoes (see note)	lime wedges to garnish

Preheat the grill. Put the swordfish steaks in the grill pan and brush with the olive oil. Sprinkle with seasoning and the juice of one of the limes. Grill the steaks under a high heat for 5–8 minutes, depending upon thickness. Meanwhile, make the salsa: chop the tomatoes roughly and the olives and onion finely. Mix together thoroughly with the coriander or parsley and some seasoning. Serve with the grilled fish and garnish with lime wedges.

NOTES AND TIPS
✦ *You can add fresh red chilli, de-seeded and chopped, to the salsa if you like.*
✦ *There is no need to skin the tomatoes, but if you prefer them skinned, cut a cross in the stalk end of each one and blanch in boiling water for 1 minute. Drain, then peel off the skins.*

Cod with a Crunchy Bacon Topping

SERVES 2

CALORIES PER PORTION: 265	PROTEIN: HIGH
TOTAL FAT PER PORTION: 6 g	CARBOHYDRATE: ★
SATURATED FAT PER PORTION: 2.5 g	FIBRE: ★

IF you find plain-cooked white fish boring (which it shouldn't be, anyway, if the fish is fresh, of good quality and well cooked), give this a try. As cod is so low in fat and calories we can afford a little indulgence in the form of bacon and cheese!

100 g (3½ oz) waxy potato, peeled	salt and freshly ground black pepper
2 thin rashers extra-lean back bacon (about 50 g/ 2 oz total weight)	I small clove garlic, crushed
	I teaspoon chopped fresh parsley
2 thick cod fillets (about 200 g/7 oz each)	50 g (2 oz) grated half-fat Mozzarella cheese

Cut the potato into four chunks and parboil in lightly salted water for about 5 minutes. Meanwhile, preheat the grill and grill the bacon rashers until golden. Remove from the heat and crumble or cut into small pieces. Drain the potato chunks and pat dry on absorbent kitchen paper, then grate them on a coarse grater. Season the fish fillets and put them on foil in the grill pan, and grill under a high heat for 3 minutes. Meanwhile, mix together the potato, bacon, garlic, parsley, some seasoning and half the cheese. Remove the grill pan from the heat and top the fish fillets with the potato mixture, pressing down well. Sprinkle the remaining cheese on top and grill for a further 4–5 minutes, or until the topping is golden, crunchy and bubbling. Serve immediately.

NOTES AND TIPS
✦ *You could use thick haddock or coley fillets instead of cod.*

Whole Trout
Steamed Chinese Style

<u>SERVES 2</u>

CALORIES PER PORTION: **366**	PROTEIN: HIGH
TOTAL FAT PER PORTION: 18g	CARBOHYDRATE: ★
SATURATED FAT PER PORTION: 4g	FIBRE: ★

I'M not normally a great fan of steamed fish, but when my friend David served this at a supper party, I was immediately convinced – it has such a clean and natural yet powerful flavour. You can either use a conventional steamer over a pan of water, or put the fish plate on a rack in a large wok and do it that way. You could even bake the fish instead, wrapped in foil with all the flavourings, or microwave it inside baking parchment. But I think the steamed version takes a lot of beating.

2 medium trout, ready for cooking	small knob fresh root ginger, peeled and thinly
1 tablespoon sesame oil	sliced
1 teaspoon salt	1 tablespoon soy sauce
4 spring onions, trimmed and halved lengthways	1 tablespoon dry sherry or sake

Score the fish twice on all sides and place on a plate which will fit inside your steamer. Rub the fish all over with half the oil and then the salt. Add the spring onions and ginger, and place the fish on the plate inside the steamer, or on a rack in a wok. Cover and steam over a high heat for 7 minutes or until the fish are cooked (don't overcook). Remove to warm serving plates. Put the soy sauce, sherry or sake and remaining sesame oil in a small saucepan and heat until very hot. Pour over the fish and serve immediately.

NOTES AND TIPS
✦ *You could use one larger whole fish (sea trout, sea bass or grouper) instead of two trout, but it needs to fit inside your cooking pan, unless you're going to bake it.*
✦ *The cooking time will vary according to the size of the fish.*
✦ *Serve the fish with rice and stir-fried carrots, mushrooms, beansprouts and green beans.*

Quick Fish and Potato Pie

SERVES 2

CALORIES PER PORTION: 450	PROTEIN: HIGH
TOTAL FAT PER PORTION: 16 g	CARBOHYDRATE: ★
SATURATED FAT PER PORTION: 6 g	FIBRE: ★★

I ADORE fish pies of all kinds – this one is both quick and healthy, and is full of vitamins, minerals and protein. For this recipe you will need some leftover boiled potatoes.

300 g (11 oz) undyed (if possible) smoked haddock fillets

a little skimmed milk

3 medium eggs, preferably free-range

350 g (13 oz) cooked floury potatoes, skins removed after cooking

salt and freshly ground black pepper

2 teaspoons butter, softened or melted

200 g (7 oz) frozen leaf spinach, thawed and well drained

¼ teaspoon freshly grated nutmeg

Preheat the oven to 200°C/400°F/Gas Mark 6. Put the haddock fillets in a pan and cover with a mixture of boiling water and skimmed milk. Bring to a simmer. Add two of the eggs to the pan (in their shells – make sure the shells are very clean). Simmer the fish and eggs together for 8 minutes. Meanwhile, mash the potato in a bowl with a little more skimmed milk, seasoning, the remaining egg and the butter. Arrange the well-drained spinach in the bottom of a shallow ovenproof dish and sprinkle on the nutmeg and some seasoning.

Remove the fish and eggs from the pan and drain the fish. Flake the fish over the spinach and season. Shell the eggs, slice and arrange over the fish. Spoon the mashed potato over the top of the fish and egg, and bake in the oven for 15–20 minutes or until the potato is turning golden and puffy. Serve immediately.

NOTES AND TIPS

✦ *If you have any fresh spinach, you could use it instead of frozen. While the fish is cooking put the leaves in a large saucepan with 1 tablespoon water, cover and cook until wilted.*

Creamed Monkfish Balti

SERVES 2

CALORIES PER PORTION: 440	PROTEIN: HIGH
TOTAL FAT PER PORTION: 25 g	CARBOHYDRATE: ★
SATURATED FAT PER PORTION: 12 g	FIBRE: ★★

FISH curries can be superb, so I don't know why we don't make them more often. You need a nice firm fish for this Balti curry – I've used monkfish but swordfish or cod would also be fine.

I tablespoon groundnut (peanut) or corn oil	300 g (11 oz) jar medium or hot Balti sauce
I small onion, finely chopped	2 tomatoes, quartered
I clove garlic, crushed	25 g (1 oz) piece creamed coconut
2 small courgettes, sliced	salt and freshly ground black pepper
75 g (3 oz) green beans, halved	I tablespoon chopped fresh coriander to garnish
350 g (13 oz) monkfish fillet, cubed	

Heat the oil in a wok or heavy pan and add the onion, garlic and courgettes. Stir-fry over a high heat for 3 minutes. Turn the heat down a little, add the beans and stir-fry for another minute. Add the fish and Balti sauce, stir, cover and simmer very gently for 10 minutes. Add the tomatoes and coconut, and simmer again, stirring gently from time to time, until the coconut has dissolved. Check the seasoning, and serve garnished with coriander.

NOTES AND TIPS
✦ *If you have any leftover potatoes around, cube them and add them to the pan with the beans if you like. They will add only 22 calories or so for 25 g (1 oz).*
✦ *Serve the curry with heated chappati at roughly 70 calories per item.*

Sin-free Fish and Chips with Tartare Sauce

SERVES 2

CALORIES PER PORTION: 460	PROTEIN: HIGH
TOTAL FAT PER PORTION: 13 g	CARBOHYDRATE: ★★
SATURATED FAT PER PORTION: 1 g	FIBRE: ★★

I LOVE fish and chips, but not when they are all soggy, heavy and loaded with fat. This version is light and delicious.

	Tartare Sauce
350 g (13 oz) potatoes	**Tartare Sauce**
salt and freshly ground black pepper	2 spring onions, finely chopped
2 medium cod fillets (about 200 g/7 oz each)	2 teaspoons capers, drained
2 tablespoons Kraft 70% fat free mayonnaise	2 teaspoons chopped fresh parsley
about 3 tablespoons rough breadcrumbs	pinch of caster sugar
Fry Light cooking spray (see page 4)	2 teaspoons Kraft 70% fat free mayonnaise
1 tablespoon corn oil	2 tablespoons natural low-fat Bio yogurt

Preheat the oven to 190°C/375°F/Gas Mark 5. Cut the potatoes into 20 or so chips and place in a saucepan. Add enough boiling water to cover and a little salt, and bring back to the boil. Reduce the heat and simmer for 5 minutes, then drain and pat dry on absorbent kitchen paper. Meanwhile, coat the fish fillets with the mayonnaise, spreading evenly all over the white parts of the fish (it doesn't matter about the undersides). Shake the breadcrumbs over the fish and press into the mayonnaise so that it is all well coated with the crumbs.

Spray a baking tray with Fry Light, and put the fish on the tray. Toss the chips in the corn oil and add them to the tray. Sprinkle with salt and pepper and bake in the oven for 20 minutes or until the fish and chips are cooked and the crumb coating and chips are golden (see note). While the fish and chips are cooking, make a tartare sauce by combining the ingredients in a small bowl. Serve the fish and chips with the tartare sauce.

NOTES AND TIPS
+ *Check the fish halfway through cooking to make sure the crumbs aren't browning too fast; if they are, lightly cover the fish pieces with two pieces of foil.*
+ *Serve with some fresh or frozen peas.*

Spiced Salmon and Lentils

<u>SERVES 2</u>

CALORIES PER PORTION: 463	PROTEIN: HIGH
TOTAL FAT PER PORTION: 23 g	CARBOHYDRATE: ★
SATURATED FAT PER PORTION: 4 g	FIBRE: ★★

SALMON and lentils go together particularly well and are an incredibly healthy combination – all that omega-3 oil in the salmon and all that lovely fibre and iron in the lentils. This is a meal that will keep hunger pangs at bay for hours for surprisingly few calories. If you can't get pre-cooked lentils you will have to add 20 minutes or so to the cooking time (see note).

I tablespoon corn or groundnut (peanut) oil	300 g (11 oz) canned chopped tomatoes
I small onion, finely chopped	100 ml (3½ fl oz) fish stock (made using a cube)
I clove garlic, crushed	salt and freshly ground black pepper
I tablespoon garam masala	2 salmon fillets (about 125 g/4½ oz each)
200 g (7 oz) ready-cooked brown or green lentils (see note)	I tablespoon half-fat crème fraîche

Heat the oil in a large non-stick sauté pan and add the onion and garlic. Stir-fry for a few minutes to soften. Add the garam masala and stir again for 1 minute or until you can smell the spicy aroma. Add the lentils, tomatoes, stock and seasoning and stir well. Bring to a simmer, then turn the heat down and cook for 5 minutes. Place the salmon fillets on top of the lentil mixture and simmer very gently for 10 minutes. Remove the salmon to heated serving plates. Stir the crème fraîche into the sauce in the pan and pour round the salmon.

NOTES AND TIPS
✦ *It is worth cooking a batch of lentils now and then. Simply simmer in a pan in plenty of water for 30 minutes or until tender. Drain and season, and use in your recipe. Freeze the surplus. If you haven't got any ready-cooked lentils, use the same weight of well-drained canned lentils.*
✦ *Serve the fish and lentils with bulghar wheat, rice or couscous.*

Hot Tuna Niçoise with a Mild Mustard Dressing

<u>SERVES 2</u>

CALORIES PER PORTION: 495	PROTEIN: HIGH
TOTAL FAT PER PORTION: 19g	CARBOHYDRATE: ★
SATURATED FAT PER PORTION: 4g	FIBRE: ★★

HERE is a nice variation on a Salade Niçoise, using fresh tuna and hot vegetables tossed in a warm and tangy dressing. Frozen tuna will do at a pinch but canned tuna *won't* do at all!

300g (11oz) new (or old, waxy) potatoes

1 medium egg

Fry Light cooking spray (see page 4)

300g (11oz) fresh tuna steaks

50g (2oz) green beans

2 Little Gem lettuces, quartered

6 cherry tomatoes or 2 medium tomatoes, quartered

3–4 spring onions, chopped

8 pitted black olives, halved

1 tablespoon chopped fresh flat-leaved parsley to garnish

Dressing

2 teaspoons runny honey

2 teaspoons wholegrain Dijon mustard (not English mustard – it's too hot)

2 tablespoons white wine

1 tablespoon olive oil

salt and fresh ground black pepper

Cook the potatoes in lightly salted boiling water for 15–20 minutes or until just cooked. Halfway through the cooking time, add the egg (making sure the shell is very clean). At the same time, heat a non-stick pan sprayed with Fry Light. When very hot, add the tuna steaks and cook for 4 minutes without turning. Meanwhile, cook the beans in a small pan of lightly salted boiling water for 3 minutes, drain and keep warm.

While the beans are cooking, arrange the lettuce quarters, and any leaves that pull off easily, on two serving plates and combine the dressing ingredients in a small bowl. Turn the tuna steaks over carefully and add the tomatoes to the edge of the pan to char slightly. Cook the tuna for another 2–3 minutes only. Meanwhile, drain the potatoes and egg. Chop the potatoes into 2 cm (³/₄ inch) chunks and shell and quarter the egg. Arrange the tuna, potatoes, egg and beans on the serving plates and top with the tomatoes, onions and olives. Tip the dressing into the sauté pan and heat for a few seconds, stirring, to warm through. Pour over the salad, garnish with the parsley and serve immediately.

Scallops with Prosciutto

<u>SERVES 2</u>

CALORIES PER PORTION: 312   PROTEIN: HIGH

TOTAL FAT PER PORTION: 12g   CARBOHYDRATE: ★

SATURATED FAT PER PORTION: 4g   FIBRE: ★★

SCALLOPS are a wonderful seafood, but sadly the frozen kind aren't worth eating and the fresh ones are expensive, so this is one of the few real luxury dishes in this book ... especially as I have combined the sweet scallops with lovely, salty prosciutto (Parma ham) from Italy, another expensive item! Still, you can always have lentils tomorrow.

12 good ready-prepared fresh scallops	12 strips prosciutto (Parma ham)
juice of 1 lime	6 small mushrooms, stems removed
freshly ground black pepper	2 teaspoons olive oil

Preheat the grill. Toss each scallop in the lime juice and season with black pepper, then wrap a slice of prosciutto around each scallop. Thread the scallops on to kebab skewers or pre-soaked bamboo satay sticks with the mushrooms. Season again with black pepper and brush with the olive oil. Grill for about 4 minutes, turning once, until the ham is crisp and golden. Serve immediately.

NOTES AND TIPS
✦ *Serve with a green salad and some rice or pasta bows.*
✦ *For a higher-calorie dish, you could serve the scallops with a sauce made by beating together one small, ripe avocado, 1 tablespoon low-fat fromage frais, some lime juice and a dash of Tabasco (hot pepper) sauce. This would work out at roughly 150 calories and 12.5g fat extra per portion – though avocado contains a high proportion of the 'good for you' fats plus vitamin E.*
✦ *A less-expensive wrapping for the scallops would be streaky bacon, but it is fattier than the ham and would take longer to cook.*

Mediterranean Seafood Medley

SERVES 2

CALORIES PER PORTION: 360	PROTEIN: HIGH
TOTAL FAT PER PORTION: 10g	CARBOHYDRATE: ★
SATURATED FAT PER PORTION: 3g	FIBRE: ★★

YOU couldn't hope to make this dish in 30 minutes if you had to prepare all the seafood from scratch. Luckily, the packs of frozen seafood cocktail that you can find in the supermarket are a very good substitute and ideal when cooking for one or two.

200g (7oz) mixed frozen seafood (usually squid, mussels, prawns), thawed (see note)

300g (11oz) fresh cod, halibut or monkfish fillet, cubed

250g (9oz) Italian tomato sauce with herbs (see note)

2 tablespoons dry white wine

200g (7oz) can mixed sweet peppers, drained and sliced

1 courgette, thinly sliced

salt and freshly ground black pepper

Put all the ingredients in a sauté pan with a lid and bring to a simmer. Lower the heat, cover and simmer for 10 minutes. Check the seasoning and serve.

NOTES AND TIPS

✦ *Don't forget to thaw the seafood slowly by putting the pack in the fridge in the morning, if you are to cook this dish in the evening. Fish and seafood hate being thawed quickly. If you do forget, put the seafood in a bowl and cover with lukewarm water. Change the water frequently until the fish is thawed. Drain and pat dry with absorbent kitchen paper. Alternatively, thaw in the microwave on low.*

✦ *If you prefer, you could use all prawns in this dish instead of the mixed seafood.*

✦ *Italian tomato sauce with herbs is available in jars from the supermarket. If you have any of your own homemade tomato sauce in the freezer you could use that instead.*

✦ *You can use small mushrooms instead of the courgette.*

✦ *Serve with some crusty bread or rice and a side salad.*

Just Mussels

<u>SERVES 2</u>

CALORIES PER PORTION: 252	PROTEIN: HIGH
TOTAL FAT PER PORTION: 10g	CARBOHYDRATE: ★
SATURATED FAT PER PORTION: 4.5g	FIBRE: ★

HERE'S a simple yet tasty recipe for a mussels supper. Mussels are an ideal food for slimmers as they are low in fat and high in protein. They also make a low-cost meal, yet most of us have never cooked a fresh mussel in our lives. Give them a try, they are very easy. All you need to do is to be sure to discard any mussel that doesn't open when cooked.

1 kg (2¼ lb) fresh mussels	bay leaf
15 g (½ oz) butter	salt
1 medium Spanish onion, finely chopped	1 teaspoon crushed peppercorns (see note)
1 clove garlic, crushed (optional)	1 tablespoon chopped fresh parsley
150 ml (5½ fl oz) dry cider	extra parsley to garnish

Prepare the mussels (unless you have bought them ready-prepared): wash them and scrub them and remove the 'beards'. Discard any that are open and will not close when tapped. Heat the butter in a large non-stick sauté pan, add the onion, and cook over a medium high heat for 5 minutes or until soft. Add the garlic, if using, and stir for 1 minute. Add the rest of the ingredients, except the mussels, and bring to a fast simmer. Add the mussels, put the lid on the pan and cook for about 5 minutes, stirring occasionally. When the mussels have opened (throw away any that don't open), remove them from the pan with a slotted spoon and place on warmed serving plates. Boil the cider sauce to reduce a little, then pour over the mussels. Garnish with extra parsley.

NOTES AND TIPS
✦ *Serve with some crusty bread and follow with a salad.*
✦ *Crush the peppercorns in some greaseproof paper or foil, using a rolling pin. If you haven't got time, just use freshly ground black pepper from a mill instead.*

Thai Prawn Sizzle

<u>SERVES 2</u>

CALORIES PER PORTION: 273	PROTEIN: HIGH
TOTAL FAT PER PORTION: 8 g	CARBOHYDRATE: ★
SATURATED FAT PER PORTION: I g	FIBRE: ★★

AN ideal quick supper when you feel like a real taste blast. Walk quickly past the Indian take-away and make this instead.

2 teaspoons groundnut (peanut) oil	½ teaspoon ground coriander
I medium yellow pepper, de-seeded and cut into I cm (½ inch) pieces	½ teaspoon Sambal Oelek (hot chilli paste)
I clove garlic, chopped	400 g (14 oz) large prawns (preferably uncooked), peeled
small knob fresh root ginger, peeled and sliced	2 teaspoons Thai fish sauce
I stalk lemon grass, crushed with a rolling pin or ½ teaspoon dried lemon grass	2 teaspoons Teriyake marinade or light soy sauce
6 spring onions, trimmed and halved lengthways	I generous teaspoon runny honey
I teaspoon sesame oil	2 teaspoons yellow bean sauce
½ teaspoon crushed cumin seed	I tablespoon coconut milk (see note)
	fresh coriander leaves to garnish

Heat the groundnut oil in a wok or large non-stick frying pan and stir-fry the yellow pepper for 2 minutes or until softened. Add the garlic, ginger, lemon grass and spring onions, and stir again for 1 minute. Add the rest of the ingredients, except the coconut milk, and stir for a few minutes until the prawns are pink and cooked. Add a little water if the mixture gets very dry, but this isn't a very liquid curry. Serve immediately, with the coconut milk drizzled over, and garnished with coriander leaves.

NOTES AND TIPS
✦ *If you have to use pre-cooked prawns, don't put them in the pan with the rest of the ingredients as above. Instead, stir-fry the spices, sauces, etc., for a few minutes and then simply add the cooked prawns for a minute to heat through at the end.*
✦ *Fresh lemon grass is wonderfully fragrant and often available in supermarkets, delicatessens or specialist stores. If you can't get it, all supermarkets sell dried lemon grass.*
✦ *Serve with Thai fragrant rice and a mixed leaf and herb salad.*

Crab Cakes with Raita Sauce

<u>SERVES 2</u>

CALORIES PER PORTION: 250	PROTEIN: HIGH
TOTAL FAT PER PORTION: 10g	CARBOHYDRATE: ★
SATURATED FAT PER PORTION: 1g	FIBRE: ★

LAST year it was salmon cakes; this year crab cakes are all the thing. Never mind, I don't mind following fashion as long as the food tastes good – and these do!

meat from 1 large or 2 small dressed crabs	dash of Tabasco (hot pepper) sauce
1 teaspoon lemon or lime juice	Fry Light cooking spray (see page 4)
2 teaspoons Kraft 70% fat free mayonnaise	**Raita Sauce**
1 teaspoon French mustard	2 tablespoons natural low-fat Bio yogurt
2 teaspoons finely chopped fresh parsley	1 tomato, de-seeded and chopped
1 shallot or 2 spring onions, finely chopped	2 cm (¾ inch) piece cucumber, chopped
about 25g (1 oz) breadcrumbs	a few coriander leaves
salt and freshly ground black pepper	

In a bowl, combine the crab meat with all the other ingredients, except the cooking spray, using enough breadcrumbs to form a firm, but not dry, mixture. Form into four cakes. Heat a non-stick frying pan sprayed with cooking spray, and cook the crab cakes for 4 minutes on each side or until nicely golden. Meanwhile, make the sauce by combining the yogurt, tomato, cucumber and coriander. Serve the cakes with the sauce.

NOTES AND TIPS
✦ *Serve with a green salad.*

OPPOSITE: Spiced Salmon and Lentils (page 68)

OPPOSITE PAGE 75: Rigatoni with Goat's Cheese and Aubergines (page 100)

CHAPTER SEVEN

VEGETABLES AND DAIRY

I reckon I am the world's greatest vegetable fan. I can think of nothing more sad than going out to one of those *nouvelle* French restaurants and paying a fortune to be served a meal with *nothing* for veggies apart from perhaps a solo sprig of spinach or a couple of minuscule baby carrots. And I can hardly believe that, until I became a 'grown up' (whenever that was!), I didn't much like vegetables at all, with the exception of runner beans. And I know I'm not alone in this.

On the other hand, it's not so surprising when you think that many of us came from homes where the only vegetables we saw on a regular basis were cabbage, sprouts, cauliflower and carrots, which when sighted were almost always a greyish, disintegrating soggy mess.

So aren't we lucky now? One of my favourite things is a roasting tin filled with chunks of butternut squash, swede, sweet potato, carrot and red onions, all brushed with olive oil, seasoned and baked. Bliss! Yet despite the mass of fabulous, colourful, flavourful and healthy vegetables now widely available throughout the year, we still don't make enough of them or with them. You don't have to be vegetarian to appreciate non-meat main courses when they taste great and are completely satisfying – as the recipes in this chapter will, I hope, prove to you.

And, for slimmers, of course vegetarian meals can be an excellent choice. They tend to be high in fibre and many are low in saturated fat. But just one word of caution: go easy on high-fat dairy additions such as Cheddar or cream cheese, eggs and whole milk. These *are* high-fat products, containing more fat, calories and (in the case of eggs) cholesterol than many meats, which is why many dairy-eating vegetarians aren't getting as healthy a diet as they think they are! Instead, use other sources of protein some of the time, such as lentils or beans, or tofu (a soya product) or Quorn, all of which contain no saturated fat and also contain fibre. Or use lower-fat dairy produce, such as half-fat hard cheeses, fromage frais and skimmed milk, in your vegetarian cooking. I do think eggs are worth including in your recipes sometimes, though, because they contain so many other nutrients as well as protein – they are rich in iron and many vitamins.

Creamed Aubergine and Mushroom Sauté

SERVES 2

CALORIES PER PORTION: 215	PROTEIN: MEDIUM
TOTAL FAT PER PORTION: 14 g	CARBOHYDRATE: ★
SATURATED FAT PER PORTION: 4 g	FIBRE: ★★

AUBERGINES are one of my favourite vegetables and they don't need to be cooked in gallons of oil, as they often are.

I medium aubergine	I teaspoon chopped fresh thyme
1½ tablespoons olive oil	200 g (7 oz) fresh just-ripe tomatoes
200 g (7 oz) flat mushrooms, sliced	50 ml (2 fl oz) half-fat crème fraîche
I small onion, finely chopped	50 ml (2 fl oz) low-fat set natural Bio yogurt
salt and freshly ground black pepper	50 ml (2 fl oz) low-fat fromage frais
I teaspoon chopped fresh oregano	

Cut the aubergine into cubes and blanch in a pan of boiling water for 2 minutes. Drain and dry on absorbent kitchen paper. Heat ½ tablespoon of the oil in a sauté pan and stir-fry the mushrooms over a high heat for 2 minutes. Remove and keep warm. Add another ½ tablespoon oil to the pan and stir-fry the aubergines for 3 minutes. Add to the mushrooms to keep warm. Heat the remaining oil in the pan, add the onion and stir-fry over a very high heat for 2 minutes or until sizzling and golden. Stir into the aubergine mixture with the seasoning and herbs. Slice the tomatoes and dry-fry over medium heat for a few minutes until soft, then spoon around the edges of the serving plates. Season with salt and pepper. Mix together the crème fraîche, yogurt and fromage frais, and add to the pan. Heat gently, stirring for a minute to heat through. Put the aubergine mixture in the centre of the serving plates and pour the crème mixture over. Serve immediately.

NOTES AND TIPS

✦ *This dish is nice served with warmed pitta breads or chappatis, or with rice.*

✦ *If you feel like an extra treat, you could grate some half-fat Mozzarella over the dish (if it is a heatproof one) and flash under a hot grill until the cheese is bubbling. This adds 50 calories and 3 g fat per 25 g (1 oz) Mozzarella.*

Spinach and Cheese Burgers

<u>SERVES 2</u>

CALORIES PER PORTION: 400	PROTEIN: HIGH
TOTAL FAT PER PORTION: 18 g	CARBOHYDRATE: ★★
SATURATED FAT PER PORTION: 6 g	FIBRE: ★★★

SPINACH and cheese are a lovely combination. For these burgers use fresh not frozen spinach.

450 g (1 lb) small fresh spinach leaves	25 g (1 oz) grated Parmesan cheese
1 tablespoon olive oil	1 egg, beaten
1 medium onion, finely chopped	dash of lemon juice
about 75 g (3 oz) fresh breadcrumbs (see note)	¼ teaspoon freshly grated nutmeg
25 g (1 oz) grated half-fat mature Cheddar-style cheese	salt and freshly ground black pepper
	Fry Light cooking spray (see page 4)

Put the spinach in a saucepan with 1 tablespoon water, cover and cook until wilted. Drain well and chop. If the spinach seems too moist, sandwich between absorbent kitchen paper to squeeze out more moisture. Heat the oil in a sauté pan and cook the onion over a medium heat for 6–8 minutes or until soft. In a bowl, combine the onion and spinach with the rest of the ingredients, except the cooking spray, and lightly form the mix into small burgers (you should make six altogether). Reheat the sauté pan and, if necessary, spray with Fry Light (there might be enough oil left in the pan to dispense with this). Add the burgers and cook for about 2 minutes on each side or until brown.

NOTES AND TIPS

✦ *These burgers go well with a homemade tomato sauce (see next recipe).*

✦ *The weight of the breadcrumbs is only approximate; you need enough to make firm, but not overfirm, patties, and white crumbs work better than brown.*

Tomato Sauce

SERVES 4

CALORIES PER PORTION: 79	PROTEIN: MEDIUM
TOTAL FAT PER PORTION: 4 g	CARBOHYDRATE: ★★
SATURATED FAT PER PORTION: 0.5 g	FIBRE: ★★

YOU should always have some homemade tomato sauce in the fridge or freezer — it is useful in so many dishes as well as for a side sauce which can be quickly jazzed up with all kinds of additions.

I tablespoon olive oil	I tablespoon tomato purée
I medium Spanish onion, finely chopped	I teaspoon sun-dried tomato purée
450 g (I lb) fresh ripe plum tomatoes *or* 425 g (15 oz) can Italian plum tomatoes	pinch of brown sugar
	dash of lemon juice
I good clove garlic, finely chopped	I teaspoon chopped fresh herbs (see note)
about 100 ml (3½ fl oz) passata	salt and freshly ground black pepper

Heat the oil in a non-stick saucepan and add the onion. Cook over a medium heat for 10 minutes or until soft. Meanwhile, if using fresh tomatoes, make a cross with a sharp knife in the stalk end of each and blanch them in boiling water for 1 minute. Drain and peel away the skin. Cut in half and press out the seeds. Chop the tomatoes on a plate so that you retain all the juice. When the onions are soft, add the garlic and stir-fry for 1–2 minutes. Add the rest of the ingredients, including the tomatoes with their juice, stir well and simmer, uncovered, for 15 minutes (longer if you have time), stirring occasionally, until you have a rich sauce.

NOTES AND TIPS
✦ *You can add a little water if the sauce seems too thick at any stage.*
✦ *For herbs, you could use basil or thyme, or a mix of Mediterranean herbs such as oregano, thyme and tarragon. Or you could omit the herbs if freezing, and add whatever herbs are suitable for the dish you are making at a later stage, when you thaw and reheat.*
✦ *You can spice up the sauce with the addition of some Tabasco (hot pepper) sauce or Sambal Oelek (hot chilli paste).*

Summer Vegetable Gratin

<u>SERVES 2</u>

CALORIES PER PORTION: 240	PROTEIN: HIGH
TOTAL FAT PER PORTION: 9 g	CARBOHYDRATE: ★★
SATURATED FAT PER PORTION: 3 g	FIBRE: ★★

A QUICK gratin, reminiscent of winter oven-bakes but lighter; ideal for using up a glut of courgettes in the garden or for when they are at their cheapest in the shops.

I small onion, chopped	100 g (3½ oz) baby sweetcorn cobs, halved
I small clove garlic, chopped	salt and freshly ground black pepper
2 teaspoons olive oil	fresh basil leaves, chopped
400 g (14 oz) can chopped tomatoes	I teaspoon thickening granules
300 g (11 oz) small tender courgettes, sliced	50 g (2 oz) reduced-fat Cheddar-style cheese
100 g (3½ oz) small mushrooms, halved or left whole	25 g (1 oz) breadcrumbs

Put the onion and garlic in a non-stick frying pan with the oil, heat and stir-fry for 3 minutes or until softened. Add the tomatoes and all the vegetables with some seasoning, bring to a simmer, cover and cook for 15 minutes, adding a little water or vegetable stock if the mix gets too dry. Preheat the grill 5 minutes before the end of the cooking time. When the courgettes are tender but still firm, add the basil and thickening granules and stir until the sauce thickens slightly. Check the seasoning and pile the mix into a heatproof serving dish. Mix the cheese and breadcrumbs and sprinkle over the top, then flash under the grill until the topping is golden and the cheese melted.

NOTES AND TIPS

◆ *You could use fresh tender tiny peas or broad beans (with their outer skins removed unless very small) instead of the corn if you like.*

◆ *For a heartier meal, you could add chunks of Quorn to the dish with the vegetables, adding about 20 calories for each 25 g (1 oz), or some ready-cooked, canned lentils at 25 calories per 25 g (1 oz).*

Bombay Vegetable Curry

<u>SERVES 2</u>

CALORIES PER PORTION: 240	PROTEIN: HIGH
TOTAL FAT PER PORTION: 8g	CARBOHYDRATE: ★★★
SATURATED FAT PER PORTION: 1g	FIBRE: ★★★

POTATOES, cauliflower and aubergine lend themselves particularly well to a meatless curry. They are chunky and flavoursome, and although I do eat meat, it is dishes like this that have helped me to cut down a lot.

200 g (7 oz) potatoes	½ teaspoon each of ground cardamom, ginger and turmeric
1 tablespoon corn or groundnut (peanut) oil	
1 red onion, chopped	200 g (7 oz) can chopped tomatoes
1 clove garlic, chopped	50 g (2 oz) frozen peas
1 medium aubergine	salt and freshly ground black pepper
150 g (5½ oz) cauliflower florets	200 ml (7 fl oz) vegetable stock
1 teaspoon ground coriander seed	2 tablespoons natural low-fat Bio yogurt
1 teaspoon ground cumin seed	1 teaspoon whole cumin or caraway seeds to garnish

Put some water on to boil in the kettle. Peel the potatoes, if necessary, and cut into smallish chunks. Put the boiling water and the potatoes in a saucepan with a little salt, and simmer for 10 minutes or until just tender. Meanwhile, heat the oil in a non-stick frying pan and add the onion and garlic. Fry over a medium heat for 5 minutes or until soft and just turning golden. Meanwhile, cut the aubergine into 1 cm (½ inch) slices, and then cut the slices in half. Cut the cauliflower into small florets.

Three minutes before the end of the potato cooking time, add the aubergine and cauliflower to the water, bring back to a simmer and parboil. Add all the spices to the onions and stir. Drain the vegetables well and add to the frying pan with the tomatoes, peas, seasoning and stock. Simmer, uncovered, for 15 minutes or until you have a rich sauce. Just before serving, stir the yogurt lightly into the curry and sprinkle the whole seeds over.

NOTES AND TIPS
✦ *If you like a hotter curry, add some ground chilli powder or flakes, and/or increase the quantity of the other spices.*

✦ *If you don't want the bother of adding all the separate spices to the pan, use 2 teaspoons (or to taste) mild curry powder. Don't use curry powder that has been around for ages. Spices, once ground, should be used within weeks, preferably days, and kept in an airtight jar in a cool, dark place (not on the kitchen shelf).*

✦ *For more protein, add some canned ready-cooked chickpeas to the dish with the vegetables, adding 25 calories per 25 g (1 oz) and little fat.*

Rustic Vegetable Rosti

SERVES 2

CALORIES PER PORTION: 200	PROTEIN: HIGH
TOTAL FAT PER PORTION: 8 g	CARBOHYDRATE: ★★
SATURATED FAT PER PORTION: 2 g	FIBRE: ★★

HERE'S, a dish that is a perfect light supper with just some crusty bread and a salad, or it could be a side dish with something like a grilled fish.

2 teaspoons corn oil	100 g (3½ oz) potato, peeled and grated
1 medium onion, thinly sliced	1 medium egg, preferably free-range, beaten
100 g (3½ oz) carrot, thickly grated	salt and freshly ground black pepper
100 g (3½ oz) parsnip, thickly grated	2 teaspoons very finely chopped fresh parsley
100 g (3½ oz) courgette, grated	

Heat the oil in a large non-stick frying pan and stir-fry the onion over a high heat for 3–4 minutes until charring slightly but still with a bite. Remove from the heat. Mix together the other vegetables in a bowl, then stir in the onion, beaten egg, seasoning and parsley, and combine well. Put the frying pan back on the heat and, when hot, add the vegetable mixture to it, flattening it out into a big cake. Cook for 5 minutes, then, using two spatulas, turn it over and cook over a medium heat for 5 minutes on the other side. Stick a sharp knife into the rosti to check it is cooked before serving – the outside should be golden brown and the inside tender and moist.

NOTES AND TIPS

✦ *You should be able to see the individual grated vegetables in the finished rosti.*

✦ *If the vegetables seem a bit too wet after you've grated them, dry them in a clean teatowel before adding the egg, etc.*

Stuffed Mushrooms

<u>SERVES 2</u>

CALORIES PER PORTION: 302	PROTEIN: MEDIUM
TOTAL FAT PER PORTION: 9 g	CARBOHYDRATE: ★★★
SATURATED FAT PER PORTION: 3 g	FIBRE: ★★

YOU need nice big tasty field mushrooms for this dish, and you need some leftover cooked rice or some of the ready-cooked frozen kind, otherwise you won't be able to make the dish within 30 minutes.

4 large, well-opened mushrooms (about 75 g/3 oz each)

2 teaspoons corn oil

4 spring onions, chopped

I small clove garlic, finely chopped

a little red or yellow pepper, de-seeded and finely chopped

250 g (9 oz) cooked rice (preferably yellow), thawed if frozen (see note)

I fresh tomato, halved, de-seeded and chopped

I teaspoon rice seasoning or Chinese five-spice seasoning (see note)

2 teaspoons soy sauce

2 teaspoons yellow bean sauce

2 teaspoons chopped fresh coriander or parsley

salt and freshly ground black pepper

50 g (2 oz) reduced-fat Mozzarella cheese, grated

Preheat the oven to 200°C/400°F/Gas Mark 6. Remove the stems from the mushrooms, chop the stems and reserve. Heat the oil in a non-stick frying pan, add the onions, garlic, chopped mushroom stems and red or yellow pepper, and stir over a medium heat for 3 minutes or until softened. Add the rice and all the remaining ingredients, except the cheese, and stir gently for a few minutes, adding a little water or vegetable stock if the mixture sticks. Put the mushrooms on a baking tray, fill them with the rice mixture and sprinkle the cheese over. Bake in the oven for 15 minutes or until the mushrooms are tender and the cheese melted and bubbling. Serve immediately.

NOTES AND TIPS

✦ *Frozen cooked rice will thaw very quickly in the microwave, or put it in a sieve and run warm water through it, then drain well.*

✦ *Serve with a large green salad.*

✦ *You will find rice seasoning and Chinese five-spice seasoning alongside the other spice jars in most supermarkets.*

Thai Stuffed Omelette

<u>SERVES 2</u>

CALORIES PER PORTION: 340	PROTEIN: HIGH
TOTAL FAT PER PORTION: 21 g	CARBOHYDRATE: ★
SATURATED FAT PER PORTION: 5 g	FIBRE: ★

THIS omelette is a triumph of taste over calories. It contains the latest buzz-word food, crab; vegetarians could use thinly sliced Quorn or sliced oyster mushrooms instead.

4 teaspoons oyster sauce	100 g (3½ oz) white crab meat
2 teaspoons brown sugar	1 teaspoon grated fresh root ginger
50 ml (2 fl oz) vegetable or chicken stock mixed with 1 teaspoon cornflour	2 spring onions, finely chopped
	salt and freshly ground black pepper
2 teaspoons sesame oil	2 teaspoons groundnut (peanut) oil
25 g (1 oz) mangetout, thinly sliced	4 medium eggs, preferably free-range
50 g (2 oz) beansprouts	1 teaspoon Thai fish sauce

Mix half the oyster sauce and half the sugar with the stock and cornflour mixture in a small saucepan. Simmer for 1 minute, then set aside. Heat the sesame oil in a non-stick frying pan and stir-fry the mangetout for 2 minutes. Add the beansprouts, crab, ginger, spring onions and a little salt, and stir-fry again for 2 minutes. Add the rest of the oyster sauce, and stir. Set the pan aside and keep warm.

Heat half the groundnut oil in an omelette pan, brushing it around the pan to give a very thin, even coating. While the pan is heating, beat together the eggs, fish sauce, black pepper and the rest of the sugar. When the pan is very hot, add half the egg mixture and cook until the underside is golden. Put half the crab filling in the centre and fold over the edges to make a parcel. Invert on to a serving plate using a large spatula, and pour over half the sauce. Repeat to make the second omelette, brushing the pan first with the remaining groundnut oil.

NOTES AND TIPS
✦ *Fresh crab meat is best but you could use frozen.*

Broccoli and Egg Gratin

<u>SERVES 2</u>

CALORIES PER PORTION: 450	PROTEIN: HIGH
TOTAL FAT PER PORTION: 24 g	CARBOHYDRATE: ★
SATURATED FAT PER PORTION: 9.5 g	FIBRE: ★★

THIS tasty supper is very rich in iron, calcium and most of the vitamins. Serve it with some bread and a salad to bring the total fat content down and the carbohydrate content up.

4 medium eggs, preferably free-range	pinch of mustard powder
225 g (8 oz) broccoli florets	salt and a little white pepper
25 g (1 oz) half-fat Anchor	25 g (1 oz) breadcrumbs
1 rounded tablespoon plain flour	50 g (2 oz) half-fat Cheddar-style cheese, grated
300 ml (11 fl oz) skimmed milk	

Preheat the oven to 200°C/400°F/Gas Mark 6. Cook the eggs in boiling water for 8 minutes. Meanwhile, in a separate pan, boil the broccoli in lightly salted water for 3 minutes or until barely cooked, then drain and transfer to an ovenproof dish. While the eggs finish cooking, heat the 'butter' in a non-stick saucepan until melted, then add the flour and stir for 2 minutes. Gradually stir in the milk until you have a smooth sauce, then add the mustard and seasoning. When the eggs are cooked, drain and rinse in cold water, then shell and quarter them. Arrange with the broccoli in the ovenproof dish. Pour the sauce over. Mix together the breadcrumbs and cheese, and sprinkle over the top. Bake in the oven for 15 minutes or until the crumbs are golden and the cheese melted.

NOTES AND TIPS

✦ *If you happen to have any leftover canned pimientos (sweet peppers) around, you could slice them and add them to the ovenproof dish with the eggs; they go very well for 10 calories or so per 25 g (1 oz).*

Pepperoni Frittata

SERVES 2

CALORIES PER PORTION: 320	PROTEIN: HIGH
TOTAL FAT PER PORTION: 23 g	CARBOHYDRATE: ★
SATURATED FAT PER PORTION: 6 g	FIBRE: ★★

FRITTATAS are a kind of Italian quiche without the pastry, and are very easy to make.

1 tablespoon corn oil	25 g (1 oz) ready-sliced mini pepperoni (see note)
1 small onion, thinly sliced	4 medium eggs, preferably free-range
1 small red pepper and 1 small yellow pepper, de-seeded and thinly sliced	1 tablespoon chopped fresh parsley
	salt and freshly ground black pepper

Preheat the grill. Heat the oil in an 18 cm (7 inch) non-stick frying pan and stir-fry the onion and peppers for 5 minutes or until soft and the onion is just turning golden. Add the pepperoni and stir-fry for another 2–3 minutes. Beat the eggs with the parsley and seasoning and add a spoonful of cold water. Pour the egg mixture into the pan over the pepper mixture, with the heat at medium high. When the underside of the frittata is set, pop the frying pan under the grill to set the top. Cut in half and serve.

NOTES AND TIPS
✦ *Serve with salad and bread.*
✦ *The pepperoni is the kind used to top a pizza, and is usually sold in small packs with the cooked meats in your supermarket. Alternatively, you could slice a Peperami stick and use that.*

Eggs Florentine

<u>SERVES 2</u>

CALORIES PER PORTION: 393	PROTEIN: HIGH
TOTAL FAT PER PORTION: 20 g	CARBOHYDRATE: ★
SATURATED FAT PER PORTION: 9 g	FIBRE: ★★

THIS is one of my favourite egg dishes. It is real nursery food; everything is so melted and soft!

450 g (1 lb) baby spinach, ready-washed and prepared	salt and a little white pepper
	pinch of mustard powder
25 g (1 oz) half-fat Anchor	50 g (2 oz) half-fat Cheddar-style cheese
1 rounded tablespoon plain flour	2 large eggs, preferably free-range
350 ml (13 fl oz) skimmed milk	1 tablespoon grated Parmesan cheese

Preheat the oven to 180°C/350°F/Gas Mark 4. Put the spinach in a large saucepan with 1 tablespoon water, cover and cook over a medium heat until wilted. Drain, chop lightly if necessary, and divide between two individual gratin dishes, spreading the spinach evenly all over the base of each dish. Melt the 'butter' in a non-stick saucepan and stir in the flour. Cook for 2 minutes over a medium heat, then slowly add the milk, stirring, until you have a smooth sauce. Add the seasoning, mustard and Cheddar-style cheese, and stir. Make a well in each of the spinach bases and break an egg into each, taking care not to break the yolks. Pour the cheese sauce over the top, covering the eggs and spinach completely, and sprinkle on the grated Parmesan. Bake in the centre of the oven for 15 minutes or until the egg whites are just set (don't overcook). Serve immediately.

NOTES AND TIPS

✦ *Serve with some French, dark rye or ciabatta bread.*

✦ *Yes, it is difficult to find out whether or not the eggs are cooked without spoiling the dish. What I do is decide which one I am going to eat and carefully spoon aside some of the sauce over the egg to have a peek. Generally speaking, unless your oven temperature is way out, 15 minutes will be fine.*

✦ *This dish contains lightly cooked eggs and might not be suitable for the elderly, the young, and pregnant women, who might prefer to avoid the slight risk of salmonella being present in the eggs.*

Pancakes with Mushroom Cheese Filling

<u>SERVES 2</u>

CALORIES PER PORTION: 450	PROTEIN: HIGH
TOTAL FAT PER PORTION: 24 g	CARBOHYDRATE: ★
SATURATED FAT PER PORTION: 9 g	FIBRE: ★★

MUSHROOMS are wonderful for slimmers – very low in calories yet quite substantial. Because mushrooms are so low in calories, the overall fat content of this recipe seems comparatively high, so make sure that the rest of the meals you have on the day you cook this are proportionately low in fat.

50 g (2 oz) plain flour	450 g (1 lb) mixed fresh mushrooms, e.g. chestnuts and shiitake, sliced
pinch of salt	
1 small egg	salt and freshly ground black pepper
75 ml (3 fl oz) skimmed milk	1 tablespoon finely chopped fresh parsley
75 ml (3 fl oz) water	200 ml (7 fl oz) 8% fat fromage frais
1½ tablespoons corn oil	50 g (2 oz) reduced-fat soft cheese with garlic

To make the pancake batter, sift the flour and salt together into a mixing bowl and break the egg into it. Beat the egg into the flour, gradually adding the milk mixed with the water until you have a smooth, thin batter.

Heat half the oil in a non-stick frying pan, add the mushrooms, seasoning and parsley, and stir-fry over a high heat for 3 minutes or until the mushrooms are golden and quite dry. Turn the heat right down and add the fromage frais and soft cheese to the pan. Leave to melt while you make the pancakes.

Heat an omelette pan brushed with a quarter of the remaining oil over a high heat. When very hot, add enough batter to coat the base of the pan, swirling it around to cover the whole surface. After a minute, lift the pancake with a spatula and look at the base. When it is flecked golden, turn the pancake over using the spatula and cook the other side for a further minute. Remove the pancake to a warm plate and cook three more in the same way, brushing the pan with oil each time and making sure the pan gets really hot again. When the pancakes are cooked, stir the mushroom cream mixture, check the seasoning and put a quarter of the mixture on one half of each of the pancakes. Fold each pancake over the mixture and serve.

CHAPTER EIGHT

RICE AND OTHER GRAINS

No slimmer's storecupboard should be without a good selection of rices and other grains, such as bulghar wheat and couscous. Grains are very good at filling your tum for few calories and virtually no fat. People think of rice as fattening, but if you exercise a modicum of portion control and eat grains in a sensible way (i.e., not with a vindaloo curry from the take-away swimming in visible spoonfuls of oil, for example!), then grains are great. They contain fibre, plenty of carbohydrate, and vitamins and minerals (especially the whole grain varieties such as brown rice). They also cook quite quickly – you can even get quick-cook brown rice now, instead of having to wait 45 minutes or so for the old type to get tender.

My favourite rice dishes are 'composites', things like paellas, pilaffs and risottos where everything is cooked in one pan. Simple, quick and delicious. At one time I wasn't a great fan of either bulghar wheat or couscous (also a wheat grain) but since I discovered how much more tasty they are when soaked in stock rather than water, I eat them frequently. For no-time-to-spare cooks they are ideal as, like noodles, they are ready to eat very quickly.

Don't forget to use grains, too, in your soups and casseroles, for extra fibre, filling power and 'bite'. The packs of mixed grains are delicious used this way.

Chicken, Rice and Chickpeas

<u>SERVES 2</u>

CALORIES PER PORTION: 639

TOTAL FAT PER PORTION: 20.5 g

SATURATED FAT PER PORTION: 5.5 g

PROTEIN: HIGH

CARBOHYDRATE: ★★

FIBRE: ★★

I ADORE chickpeas, but it is easier than it should be to buy dried ones that seem to need about 48 hours cooking and *still* end up tough. Get round this problem by using canned ones; if you only want a small amount, it saves a lot of messing about. You'll love the nutty, floury taste of the 'peas' in this Mediterranean-style dish, which is, by the way, a meal for a very hungry person. If you're not ravenous, a half portion will suffice!

I tablespoon olive oil

2 skinned chicken breast fillets or 4 skinned and boned chicken thighs

2 chorizo sausages

I medium Spanish onion, finely chopped

150 g (5½ oz) canned chickpeas (drained weight; a 200 g/7 oz can will yield roughly this amount)

100 g (3½ oz) drained, canned pimientos (sweet red peppers), each cut into two

I saffron rice stock cube (see note)

150 ml (5½ fl oz) boiling water

freshly ground black pepper

I tablespoon chopped fresh parsley or chervil

100 g (3½ oz) long-grain rice

Heat the oil in a non-stick sauté pan. While the oil is heating, cut the chicken breasts into four pieces each, or each thigh into two, and slice the chorizos. Add the onion to the pan and stir-fry for 2–3 minutes or until softened, then add the chicken and chorizo pieces, stir and cook until lightly browned. Turn down the heat a little, add the chickpeas and peppers, and stir. Mix the saffron cube well into the boiling water and add to the pan with the pepper and parsley or chervil. Bring to a simmer, turn the heat down again, cover and simmer for 15–20 minutes. Meanwhile, cook the rice in a saucepan of boiling water for about 15 minutes or until almost cooked. Drain the rice if necessary, stir into the sauté pan and mix well with the rest of the ingredients, adding more water if required to give a moist, but not wet, finished dish.

NOTES AND TIPS

✦ *Saffron rice stock cubes are made by Knorr. If you can't get them, use a sachet of real saffron and chicken stock instead of water.*

Prawn and Chicken Creole

<u>SERVES 2</u>

CALORIES PER PORTION: 510	PROTEIN: HIGH
TOTAL FAT PER PORTION: 8.5 g	CARBOHYDRATE: ★★★
SATURATED FAT PER PORTION: 1.5 g	FIBRE: ★★

THIS is a kind of American-style risotto, I suppose, though it is less creamy than a risotto and more spicy. It makes a nice change, anyway, and, in common with all the dishes in this chapter, has the advantage of needing no accompaniments unless you want to serve salad.

I tablespoon corn oil	200 g (7 oz) can chopped tomatoes
200 g (7 oz) skinned and boned chicken breast, cut into chunks	125 g (4½ oz) American long-grain rice
	200 ml (7 fl oz) chicken stock (see note)
I medium red onion, chopped	2 teaspoons chopped fresh oregano or I teaspoon dried
I small red pepper and I small green or yellow pepper, de-seeded and chopped	100 g (3½ oz) peeled cooked prawns, fresh or thawed if frozen
I large clove garlic, chopped	
I teaspoon red chilli flakes (or to taste)	

Heat the oil in a large non-stick sauté pan, add the chicken and cook for 1–2 minutes or until brown. Add the onion, peppers and garlic, and stir for a few minutes or until softened. Add the rest of the ingredients, except the prawns, and bring to a simmer. Turn the heat down, cover and simmer for 20 minutes or until the rice has absorbed much of the liquid. Add the prawns and heat through for a minute before serving.

NOTES AND TIPS
✦ *The amount of stock given is approximate, and will depend upon various factors. Check the dish once, 5 minutes or so before the end of the cooking time, and if it looks too dry, add a little more stock and stir.*

Kedgeree

SERVES 2

CALORIES PER PORTION: 467	PROTEIN: HIGH
TOTAL FAT PER PORTION: 16.5 g	CARBOHYDRATE: ★★
SATURATED FAT PER PORTION: 5 g	FIBRE: ★★

EGGS and rice are one of my favourite combinations – add a hint of curry and some tasty smoked fish and you almost have heaven!

2 medium eggs	2 teaspoons mild curry powder (or to taste)
500 ml (18 fl oz) fish stock (see note)	100 g (3½ oz) basmati rice
175 g (6 oz) undyed (if possible) smoked haddock fillets	50 g (2 oz) small peas, fresh or thawed if frozen
	1 tablespoon chopped fresh parsley
2 teaspoons corn oil	salt and freshly ground black pepper
2 teaspoons butter	lemon wedges to garnish
1 medium onion, finely chopped	

Boil the eggs for 8 minutes, drain and cool under cold running water. Meanwhile, heat the fish stock in a frying pan, add the haddock fillets and simmer for 3–4 minutes. Drain, reserving the stock, and flake.

While the eggs are boiling and the fish is simmering, heat the oil and butter in a non-stick frying pan and sauté the onion over a medium high heat for 8–10 minutes or until soft and turning golden. Stir the curry powder into the pan and cook for 1 minute. Stir in the rice, then add the reserved fish stock. Bring to a simmer and simmer for 10 minutes. Add the haddock and peas to the pan, stir, and simmer again for 10 minutes, stirring once or twice. Add extra water or stock if the mixture becomes too dry before the rice is tender.

Meanwhile, shell and quarter the eggs. When the rice is tender and the stock absorbed, stir in the parsley and black pepper, and taste to see if you need to add any salt. Finally, add the eggs and serve, garnished with lemon wedges.

NOTES AND TIPS
✦ *Very gentle cooking is the secret of kedgeree, otherwise you will end up with all the liquid evaporated, the pan burnt and the rice still tough in the centre!*
✦ *Fresh fish stock is available from the chilled cabinet of most supermarkets. Otherwise, use half a fish stock cube in water.*

Quick Lamb Biryani

<u>SERVES 2</u>

CALORIES PER PORTION: 633	PROTEIN: HIGH
TOTAL FAT PER PORTION: 28.5g	CARBOHYDRATE: ★★
SATURATED FAT PER PORTION: 10g	FIBRE: ★★

BIRYANI is a delectable Indian combination of meat, spices, yogurt and rice, and can take hours to prepare and cook. This quick version retains the spirit of the dish but is much quicker and simpler. It is higher in fat and calories than most of the recipes in this book, but is much, much lower in both than you could get in an Indian restaurant or take-away. And even slimmers can have a treat now and then!

1½ tablespoons corn or groundnut (peanut) oil	250g (9oz) fillet of lamb, cut into strips
1 medium onion, thinly sliced	about 400ml (¾ pint) lamb stock (see note)
1 small aubergine, chopped quite small	125g (4½oz) quick-cook basmati rice
1 clove garlic, chopped	125g (4½oz) natural low-fat bio Yogurt
1 teaspoon each of grated fresh root ginger, ground coriander seed and ground cumin seed	salt and freshly ground black pepper
½ teaspoon each of ground cardamon, cloves and cinnamon	fresh coriander or parsley leaves to garnish

Heat 1 tablespoon of the oil in a large, lidded, non-stick sauté pan and stir-fry the onion and aubergine over a high heat for 2–3 minutes or until softened and golden. Add the garlic and all the spices, and stir for 1 minute until you can smell the spicy aroma, then add the remaining oil and the lamb, and stir-fry for 2–3 minutes. Add the lamb stock and rice, stir, cover and simmer for 15–20 minutes or until most of the stock is absorbed and the lamb and rice are tender. Stir in the yogurt and seasoning, and serve garnished with coriander or parsley.

NOTES AND TIPS
✦ *You might need to add more stock or water towards the end of the cooking time.*
✦ *Fresh lamb stock is available from the chilled cabinet in most supermarkets or you can make some up using a lamb stock cube.*

Mushroom and Artichoke Risotto

SERVES 2

CALORIES PER PORTION: 378	PROTEIN: MEDIUM
TOTAL FAT PER PORTION: 10g	CARBOHYDRATE: ★★★
SATURATED FAT PER PORTION: 2.5g	FIBRE: ★★

IF you use ingredients that require little or no preparation, you can make a risotto from scratch in 30 minutes.

1 tablespoon olive oil	500 ml (18 fl oz) vegetable or chicken stock
1 medium onion, finely chopped	6 canned artichoke hearts, well drained and halved
1 large clove garlic, crushed	1 tablespoon chopped fresh parsley
300g (11 oz) small chestnut mushrooms, halved	2 tablespoons grated Parmesan cheese (about
salt and freshly ground black pepper	15g/½ oz)
125g (4½ oz) risotto rice (see note)	

Heat the oil in a large non-stick sauté pan and fry the onion and garlic for 5 minutes or until soft, stirring occasionally. Add the mushrooms and seasoning, and stir for 1 minute. Add the rice and stock, stir and bring to a simmer, then cover and simmer for 15 minutes. Add the artichoke hearts, stir and simmer for a further 5 minutes, adding extra stock or water if the mixture looks too dry – a risotto should be quite moist. Check that the rice is tender, and serve sprinkled with the parsley and cheese.

NOTES AND TIPS

✦ *This is a very simple risotto. If you have more time you could add a different variety of mushrooms; you could even soak some dried porcini and add them. For a more robust supper, you could also add diced cooked chicken or turkey.*

✦ *Don't use any rice other than proper risotto rice, otherwise you won't get the right texture.*

Nasi Goreng

<u>SERVES 2</u>

CALORIES PER PORTION: 555	PROTEIN: HIGH
TOTAL FAT PER PORTION: 14 g	CARBOHYDRATE: ★★
SATURATED FAT PER PORTION: 3 g	FIBRE: ★

THIS Indonesian rice dish is traditionally an accompaniment, but if you add enough bits and pieces to it, it becomes a meal in itself.

125 g (4½ oz) long-grain rice	I small clove garlic, crushed
2 teaspoons groundnut (peanut) oil	I small green chilli, de-seeded and chopped
I large egg, beaten with a little salt	100 g (3½ oz) peeled cooked prawns
2 teaspoons sesame oil	50 g (2 oz) crab meat
175 g (6 oz) turkey fillet, cut into strips	50 g (2 oz) beansprouts
I small carrot, cut into strips	I tablespoon soy sauce
4 spring onions, trimmed and halved lengthways	I teaspoon caster sugar

Cook the rice in 300 ml (11 fl oz) boiling salted water, covered, for about 15 minutes or until the water has been absorbed and the rice is barely tender. Meanwhile, heat an omelette pan brushed with a little of the groundnut oil and, when hot, add the egg. After 1 minute, turn and cook the other side, and then transfer the flat omelette to a chopping board and cut into thin strips. Reserve.

Heat the rest of the oils in a wok or large non-stick pan and stir-fry the turkey for 2 minutes. Add the carrot, onions, garlic and chilli, and stir-fry again for 2 minutes. If the rice is still cooking, remove the pan from the heat at this stage and wait for the rice. If the rice is cooked, add it to the pan with the rest of the ingredients and stir gently over a medium to low heat for 4–5 minutes. Serve garnished with the egg strips.

NOTES AND TIPS

◆ *You can use chicken instead of turkey if you like, or, for a vegetarian dish, use slices of Quorn or tofu.*

Saffron Couscous with Chicken

SERVES 2

CALORIES PER PORTION: 490	PROTEIN: HIGH
TOTAL FAT PER PORTION: 12g	CARBOHYDRATE: ★★★
SATURATED FAT PER PORTION: 1.5g	FIBRE: ★

I USED to think that couscous was bland – and it is, a bit, if you soak it in plain water. But use well-flavoured stock and the couscous is transformed into something definitely more-ish!

1 tablespoon olive oil	50g (2oz) sweetcorn kernels
2 skinned chicken breast fillets, each cut into 4 chunks	25g (1oz) sultanas
	1 tablespoon pine nuts
4 spring onions, chopped	6 cherry tomatoes, halved
125g (4½oz) couscous	fresh coriander leaves to garnish
1 saffron stock cube dissolved in 300ml (11fl oz) boiling water	

Heat the oil in a large frying pan and brown the chicken pieces, adding the spring onions at the last minute and stirring well. While the chicken is cooking, put the couscous in a bowl, pour the stock over it, stir and leave for a few minutes until the stock is absorbed, then add the couscous to the frying pan with the sweetcorn, sultanas, pine nuts and tomatoes. Cook over a gentle heat for 1–2 minutes, stirring from time to time. Serve garnished with coriander.

NOTES AND TIPS
✦ *Serve with a side salad.*
✦ *You can stir other vegetables into the dish if you like – cooked green beans or broad beans, for example, go very well.*

Bulghar Wheat Pilaff with Grilled Vegetables

<u>SERVES 2</u>

CALORIES PER PORTION: 380	PROTEIN: MEDIUM
TOTAL FAT PER PORTION: 8 g	CARBOHYDRATE: ★★★
SATURATED FAT PER PORTION: 1 g	FIBRE: ★★★

BULGHAR wheat is not quite so light and delicate as couscous but it is just as quick to cook and marries very well with all kinds of grilled vegetables.

1 small to medium aubergine	salt and freshly ground black pepper
1 courgette	1 tablespoon olive oil
1 red pepper and 1 yellow pepper	125 g (4½ oz) bulghar wheat
1 red onion	300 ml (11 fl oz) vegetable stock
1 large clove garlic, chopped	1 beef tomato
2 teaspoons lemon juice	1 tablespoon chopped fresh basil or parsley

Preheat the grill to high. Slice the aubergine into 1 cm (½ inch) rounds and then slice each round in half; slice the courgette lengthways into four; de-seed the peppers and cut into six or eight pieces each; peel the onion and cut into six segments. Arrange all the vegetables (but not the tomato) in the grill pan and sprinkle over the garlic, lemon juice, seasoning and oil. Put the bulghar wheat in a bowl. Boil the stock in a pan, and pour over the wheat. Leave to stand in a warm place.

Grill the vegetables for a few minutes or until turning golden and soft. Cut the tomato into four chunks and add to the grill. Turn the rest of the vegetables over and spoon over any pan juices/oil that has run off. Grill again until the vegetables and tomato are slightly charred and tender. Stir the basil or parsley into the bulghar, and serve with the vegetables on top, plus any juices left in the grilling pan.

NOTES AND TIPS

✦ *You can reheat the bulghar wheat for 30 seconds in a microwave if you haven't been able to keep it warm enough, or you can place it in a steamer over boiling water to keep hot once it has absorbed the stock.*

CHAPTER NINE

PASTA, NOODLES AND PIZZA

Ask most people whether or not they think pasta is a fattening food, and they will say, 'yes'! Those that don't may well plump for pizza as being one of the world's most sinful meals. In fact, pasta is a healthy food containing no more calories, weight for weight (cooked), than either rice or potatoes. It only becomes fattening when you add lots of high-fat ingredients to it, for example in the form of classic carbonara sauce. The same is true of pizza. The bread base is a low-fat healthy food item. It only becomes a dieter's nightmare when topped with all manner of very high-fat things from full-fat Mozzarella to beef and pepperoni.

In this chapter I provide a selection of what I hope you will find mouthwatering alternatives. Some of the pasta dishes contain reasonable amounts of fat, but in the form of 'good for you' oils, such as olive oil, olives, pine nuts, anchovies and salmon. If you want pasta with that creamy taste that you get with egg-and-cream-rich carbonara sauce, then choose fromage frais – the 8 per cent fat version is smooth and delicious when mixed with pasta and other flavourings, for a mere 28 calories and 2 g fat per 25 g (1 oz) as opposed to double cream which has 112 calories and 12 g fat for 25 g (1 oz)! Half-fat crème fraîche is another good alternative though higher than the fromage frais in both calories and fat at 42 calories and 3.7 g fat for 25 g (1 oz).

When preparing your own pasta and pizza dishes, remember to pile as many chopped vegetables into your recipe as you can. Homemade tomato sauce is almost essential for many pasta and most pizza dishes, so make up a batch when you have some spare time (see recipe on page 78). Freeze it in portions, thaw it while your pasta is cooking, and use it as a quick sauce mixed with any vegetables or herbs you fancy for a real instant meal.

Creamy Chicken and Vegetable Pasta

<u>SERVES 2</u>

CALORIES PER PORTION: 546	PROTEIN: HIGH
TOTAL FAT PER PORTION: 20.5 g	CARBOHYDRATE: ★★
SATURATED FAT PER PORTION: 6 g	FIBRE: ★★★

THIS is a nice summer pasta dish but the vegetables do need to be firm, fresh and of top quality.

I very fresh medium courgette	150 g (5½ oz) cooked chicken (no skin), cut into strips
I very fresh medium carrot	
125 g (4½ oz) tagliatelle	2 tablespoons half-fat crème fraîche
2 teaspoons olive oil	2 tablespoons 0% fat fromage frais
100 g (3½ oz) small tender broad beans, thawed if frozen	I tablespoon fresh pesto sauce (see note)
	salt and freshly ground black pepper
I small clove garlic, crushed	fresh tarragon leaves to garnish

Put a large pan of salted water on to boil. Top and tail the courgette and carrot, then wash the courgette and peel the carrot. Using a vegetable parer, cut them lengthways into thin ribbons and blanch in a small pan of boiling water for 1 minute. Drain well.

Add the pasta to the large pan of boiling water, stir and leave to boil, uncovered, for 10 minutes or as instructed on the pack. Meanwhile, heat the oil in a large non-stick frying pan, add the broad beans and stir-fry over a medium high heat for 2 minutes. Add the carrots, courgettes, garlic and chicken, and stir-fry for 2 minutes. Set the pan aside off the heat.

Beat together the crème fraîche, fromage frais, pesto and seasoning. When the pasta is cooked, drain it. Add the crème mixture to the frying pan back on the heat and stir for 1–2 minutes, then serve the pasta with the sauce lightly stirred into it and garnished with fresh tarragon leaves.

NOTES AND TIPS

✦ *You could add peas and/or sweetcorn to this dish for extra fibre and vitamin C.*
✦ *Pesto sauce is sold in jars and tubes in most supermarkets.*

Pasta Bows with Asparagus and Bacon

<u>SERVES 2</u>

CALORIES PER PORTION: 422	PROTEIN: HIGH
TOTAL FAT PER PORTION: 12 g	CARBOHYDRATE: ★★★
SATURATED FAT PER PORTION: 4.5 g	FIBRE: ★★

YOU really need fresh asparagus for this simple dish and it is best if you use only the tips (about 7 cm/2¾ inches of the tip and stalk). Save the rest of the stalks, cook them and use them, chopped, in omelettes and stir-fries.

2 rashers extra-lean back bacon	1 clove garlic, crushed
2 teaspoons olive oil	2 tablespoons dry white wine
150 g (5½ oz) farfalle (pasta bows)	2 tablespoons half-fat single cream
12 medium asparagus tips	salt and freshly ground black pepper
1 small onion, finely chopped	2 tablespoons large flaked Parmesan cheese

Put a large pan of salted water on to boil. Meanwhile, put the bacon in a non-stick frying pan brushed with olive oil and heat first on low, then higher as the bacon begins to cook. When the pan water is boiling, add the pasta, stir and leave to boil, uncovered, for about 10 minutes or as instructed on the pack. Turn the bacon and cook on the other side. Remove it from the frying pan when it is golden, and break into small pieces. Put a small pan of lightly salted water on to boil and, when it is boiling, add the asparagus tips. Cook for 3 minutes, then drain.

Wipe out the frying pan, add any remaining olive oil to it with the onion and garlic, and stir-fry for 3 minutes. Turn the heat down low and cook for another 2–3 minutes, adding a very little water to the pan. When the pasta is cooked (it should be just tender, or *al dente*), drain it. Add the wine to the frying pan and bubble for 1 minute, then add the cream, asparagus, bacon and seasoning, and stir to heat through. Serve the pasta with the asparagus sauce lightly stirred into it and with the Parmesan flakes on top.

NOTES AND TIPS

✦ *You could use halved artichoke hearts instead of the asparagus when asparagus is out of season – canned artichoke hearts are fine.*

Rigatoni with Goat's Cheese and Aubergines

SERVES 2

CALORIES PER PORTION: 475	PROTEIN: MEDIUM
TOTAL FAT PER PORTION: 22.5 g	CARBOHYDRATE: ★★
SATURATED FAT PER PORTION: 6 g	FIBRE: ★★★

THIS is a lovely pasta dish, with a fresh-tasting sauce combining cooked and raw ingredients. Rigatoni is a thick tube pasta, rather like penne, and is ideal for robust sauces.

I large aubergine	6 cherry tomatoes, halved
I tablespoon olive oil	6 pieces sun-dried tomato, chopped
salt and freshly ground black pepper	6 pitted black olives, halved
2 fresh tomatoes, quartered	I tablespoon sun-dried tomato oil (see note)
125 g (4½ oz) rigatoni (or penne)	I tablespoon mixed chopped fresh basil and parsley
75 g (3 oz) soft goat's cheese, cut into chunks	or chervil

Preheat the grill and put a pan of salted water on to boil. Top and tail the aubergine and cut it into 1 cm (½ inch) slices, then cut the slices into quarters. Toss the aubergine pieces in a bowl with the olive oil and some seasoning, and then grill for 10 minutes, turning and adding the tomato quarters after 5 minutes. While the aubergine is cooking, add the pasta to the pan of boiling water and leave it to boil for 10 minutes or as instructed on the pack.

When the pasta is cooked (it should be just tender, or *al dente*), drain it, put it in a warmed serving bowl and stir in the goat's cheese, cherry tomatoes, sun-dried tomato pieces, olives, tomato oil, seasoning and herbs. When the aubergines are golden and soft, which should be at about the same time as the pasta is ready and you have added the cold ingredients, stir them into the pasta with the cooked tomatoes. Serve immediately.

NOTES AND TIPS

✦ *You could use Greek Feta or Halloumi cheese instead of the goat's cheese, but they aren't so soft; the goat's cheese tends to melt in the warmth of the pasta and aubergines and produces a nice hint of cream.*

✦ *For the tomato oil, just use the oil from a jar of sun-dried tomatoes in oil.*

Spaghettini with Seafood Sauce

Serves 2

Calories per portion: 460	Protein: High
Total fat per portion: 11 g	Carbohydrate: ★★★
Saturated fat per portion: 1.5 g	Fibre: ★★

This dish takes just minutes to make and has bags of flavour.

150 g (5½ oz) spaghettini	50 ml (2 fl oz) fish stock (see note on page 91)
1 tablespoon olive oil	salt and freshly ground black pepper
1 medium mild onion, finely chopped	meat from 1 dressed crab (about 225 g/8 oz),
1–2 large cloves garlic, crushed	preferably fresh *or* 225 g (8 oz) peeled cooked
400 g (14 oz) can chopped tomatoes	prawns (see note)
2 tablespoons dry white wine	fresh parsley sprigs to garnish
1 tablespoon chopped fresh parsley	

Put a pan of salted water on to boil and, when boiling, add the pasta and boil for 8 minutes, uncovered, or as instructed on the pack. Meanwhile, heat the oil in a non-stick frying pan and stir-fry the onion and garlic for 5 minutes or until soft and just turning golden. Add the tomatoes and stir again for 1–2 minutes. Add the rest of the ingredients, except the seafood and pasta, lower the heat and cook for 5 minutes. While the sauce is simmering, check the pasta and, when cooked (it should be just tender, or *al dente*), drain. Add the seafood to the frying pan, stir and serve the seafood sauce with the pasta, garnished with parsley.

Notes and tips
✦ *Crab is sweet and strong; prawns are salty and savoury and less rich – choose whichever you prefer.*

Tagliatelle with Spinach and Mint Pesto

SERVES 2

CALORIES PER PORTION: 465	PROTEIN: MEDIUM
TOTAL FAT PER PORTION: 22.5 g	CARBOHYDRATE: ★★
SATURATED FAT PER PORTION: 6 g	FIBRE: ★★

IF you're bored with basil pesto, this makes a nice change. It's a real gutsy pasta dish that is so simple to make.

125 g (4½ oz) tagliatelle	4 sun-dried tomatoes, roughly chopped, or 2
1 tablespoon pine nuts	teaspoons sun-dried tomato purée
1 generous tablespoon chopped fresh mint	1 pack washed baby spinach
1 small clove garlic, crushed	100 g (3½ oz) half-fat soft cheese with garlic and
½ teaspoon salt	herbs
1 tablespoon olive oil	

Preheat the grill. Put a pan of salted water on to boil and, when boiling, add the pasta and boil, uncovered, for 10 minutes or as instructed on the pack. Meanwhile, to make the mint pesto sauce, spread the pine nuts on a baking tray, or on foil on the grill pan, and toast under the grill for 1 minute or until golden (careful they don't burn). Put into a pestle and mortar with the mint, garlic and salt, and crush well for a minute or two, then add the olive oil and combine. If using sun-dried tomato purée you can also add this to the mint pesto now.

When the pasta is nearly cooked, put the spinach in a saucepan with 1 tablespoon of water, cover and cook over a medium high heat, stirring once or twice, until wilted. Drain the pasta (when cooked it should be just tender, or *al dente*), and toss into a warm serving bowl. Add the soft cheese, which will melt in the pasta's heat, then the spinach, tossing lightly, and the sun-dried tomatoes, if using. Spoon the mint pesto dressing over and serve immediately.

NOTES AND TIPS

✦ *Mint, parsley and other fresh herbs are easy to chop quickly and finely if you dampen them slightly and use a large, heavy chef's knife with a wide, sharp blade and heavy handle. Mind your fingers!*

Penne with Stir-Fried Mediterranean Vegetables

SERVES 2

CALORIES PER PORTION: 460	PROTEIN: MEDIUM
TOTAL FAT PER PORTION: 15.5 g	CARBOHYDRATE: ★★★
SATURATED FAT PER PORTION: 3 g	FIBRE: ★★★

THIS is a kind of ratatouille variation which looks beautiful and is very more-ish.

125 g (4½ oz) penne (pasta tubes)	I clove garlic, chopped
I medium aubergine, chopped into 2 cm (¾ inch) pieces	I courgette, thinly sliced
2 tablespoons olive oil	3–4 canned plum tomatoes
salt and freshly ground black pepper	a little passata
I Spanish onion, finely sliced	I tablespoon grated half-fat Mozzarella cheese (see note)
I red pepper and I yellow pepper, de-seeded and chopped	a few fresh basil leaves
	4 pitted black olives, chopped

Put the grill on to heat and put a pan of salted water on to boil. When the water is boiling, add the pasta and boil, uncovered, for about 12 minutes or as instructed on the pack. Meanwhile, toss the aubergine in half the olive oil, spread on a baking tray, sprinkle with a little salt and pepper, and grill for a few minutes or until golden. Turn and grill the other side.

While the aubergine is cooking, heat the rest of the oil in a large non-stick frying pan or wok and stir-fry the onion and peppers over a high heat for 5 minutes. Add the garlic and courgette, and stir-fry again for 5 minutes. Add the aubergine and tomatoes, stir, then add a little passata and some seasoning.

Drain the pasta when cooked (it should be just tender, or *al dente*). Toss in the vegetables and serve sprinkled with the cheese, basil and olives.

NOTES AND TIPS

✦ *You can buy grated half-fat Mozzarella in most supermarkets. You can freeze the re-sealable pack and just take out what you need.*

Spaghetti Puttanesca

<u>SERVES 2</u>

CALORIES PER PORTION: 422	PROTEIN: MEDIUM
TOTAL FAT PER PORTION: 15.5 g	CARBOHYDRATE: ★★★
SATURATED FAT PER PORTION: 3 g	FIBRE: ★★

A CLASSIC Italian pasta dish which is very healthy and has a marvellous, piquant, salty flavour.

150 g (5½ oz) spaghetti	2 teaspoons drained and rinsed capers (see note)
1½ tablespoons olive oil	2 tablespoons finely chopped fresh flat-leaved
4 anchovy fillets, chopped (see note)	parsley (see note)
1 clove garlic, crushed	salt and freshly ground black pepper
200 g (7 oz) can chopped tomatoes	2 tablespoons grated Parmesan or Pecorino cheese
6 pitted black olives, chopped	

Put a large pan of salted water on to boil and, when boiling, add the pasta, pushing down the ends as it softens. Boil, uncovered, for about 10 minutes or as instructed on the pack. Meanwhile, heat the oil in a non-stick frying pan, add the anchovies and garlic, and cook for 1 minute or until the garlic begins to colour. Add the tomatoes and olives, and simmer for 15 minutes, stirring from time to time. Meanwhile, when the pasta is cooked (it should be just tender, or *al dente*), drain it. Add the capers, parsley and black pepper to the sauce and taste it, adding a little salt if you want to. Serve the pasta with the sauce over it and sprinkled with the cheese.

NOTES AND TIPS
✦ *Anchovy fillets often come eight to a tin – you can wrap the rest in cling film and freeze them for another time.*
✦ *Capers are the flower heads of a wild plant. They come in brine in small jars from most supermarkets. You need to rinse them before use. They have a delicious, piquant flavour and are what gives tartare sauce its piquancy.*
✦ *If you can't get flat-leaved parsley, use chervil or ordinary parsley.*

Pasta Shells with Salmon in Saffron Cream Sauce

<u>SERVES 2</u>

CALORIES PER PORTION: 504
TOTAL FAT PER PORTION: 20 g
SATURATED FAT PER PORTION: 8.5 g

PROTEIN: HIGH
CARBOHYDRATE: ★★
FIBRE: ★★

THIS is one of my all-time favourite pasta dishes. Saffron is one of my favourite flavourings and, although it is expensive, a little goes a long way. Half quantities of this dish would be an excellent dinner-party starter.

125 g (4½ oz) conchiglie (pasta shells)	2 shallots, finely chopped
1 sachet saffron stamens	1 small clove garlic, finely chopped
50 ml (2 fl oz) hot fish or vegetable stock	2 tablespoons dry white wine
100 g (3½ oz) small broccoli florets	50 ml (2 fl oz) half-fat crème fraîche
50 g (2 oz) small peas, fresh or thawed if frozen	2 teaspoons chopped fresh dill or tarragon
15 g (½ oz) butter	salt and freshly ground black pepper
150 g (5½ oz) salmon fillet	

Put a pan of salted water on to boil and, when boiling, add the pasta. Boil, uncovered, for about 12 minutes or as instructed on the pack. Meanwhile, put the saffron in a cup with the hot stock and leave to infuse for a few minutes. Blanch the broccoli and peas in slightly salted boiling water for 2 minutes and drain.

While the vegetables are blanching, heat the butter in a non-stick frying pan, add the salmon, and cook for 2 minutes on each side, then remove from the pan and flake. Add the shallots and garlic to the pan and fry over a medium heat for 5 minutes, stirring from time to time, until they are soft and just turning golden. Add the wine and bubble for 1 minute, then add the saffron and stock, stir and cook for another 1 minute. Add the crème fraîche and dill or tarragon, season, and simmer very gently for 1 minute. Stir in the vegetables and salmon, and drain the pasta. Serve the pasta topped with the salmon sauce.

NOTES AND TIPS

✦ *If you can't get saffron stamens, use ½ teaspoon saffron powder.*

Pappardelle with Red Onion and Chorizo

SERVES 2

CALORIES PER PORTION: 582	PROTEIN: MEDIUM
TOTAL FAT PER PORTION: 26 g	CARBOHYDRATE: ★★
SATURATED FAT PER PORTION: 8 g	FIBRE: ★★★

THIS butch pasta dish includes a taste of Spain in the form of chorizo. Yes, deli sausages are quite high in fat, but because they are so flavoursome, you only need a little.

1½ tablespoons olive oil	50 ml (2 fl oz) passata
2 large red onions, cut into quarters	1 tablespoon chopped fresh flat-leaved parsley
3 chorizo sausages, cut into 2 cm (¾ inch) chunks	salt and freshly ground black pepper
50 ml (2 fl oz) dry white wine	125 g (4½ oz) pappardelle (wide ribbon pasta)
2 medium tomatoes, chopped	

Heat the oil in a large non-stick frying pan. While the oil is heating, use your fingers to separate the 'leaves' of the quartered onions. Add the onion pieces to the pan, and stir-fry over a high heat for 3 minutes. Add the sausage and stir for 1 minute, then turn the heat down to medium and leave to cook for 5 minutes more. Add the wine to the pan, bubble for a minute, then add the tomatoes, passata, parsley and seasoning, and leave to simmer for 15 minutes, stirring occasionally. Meanwhile, put a pan of salted water on to boil and, when boiling, add the pasta. Boil, uncovered, for about 12 minutes or as instructed on the pack. When the pasta is cooked (it should be just tender, or *al dente*), drain. Check the sauce seasoning and serve with the pasta.

NOTES AND TIPS
✦ *You could use penne (pasta tubes) instead of the pappardelle if you liked.*

OPPOSITE: Hot Bacon, Mushroom and Avocado Salad (page 117)

Tomato, Tuna and Chilli Pasta

SERVES 2

CALORIES PER PORTION: 443	PROTEIN: HIGH
TOTAL FAT PER PORTION: 9.5 g	CARBOHYDRATE: ★★★
SATURATED FAT PER PORTION: 2 g	FIBRE: ★★

AN easy, no-fuss supper that never fails to please.

I tablespoon olive oil	150 g (5½ oz) fusilli (pasta spirals)
I medium onion, finely chopped	150 g (5½ oz) canned tuna in brine, well drained
I clove garlic, finely chopped	and flaked
I fresh red chilli and I fresh green chilli, de-seeded	I tablespoon chopped fresh coriander leaves
and finely chopped (see note)	salt and freshly ground black pepper
200 g (7 oz) can chopped tomatoes	I tablespoon grated Parmesan cheese
2 teaspoons sun-dried tomato purée	

Heat the oil in a frying pan and stir-fry the onion, garlic and chillies for about 5 minutes or until the onions are soft. Add the tomatoes and tomato purée, and simmer for 15 minutes. Meanwhile, put a pan of salted water on to boil and, when boiling, add the pasta. Boil, uncovered, for 12 minutes or as instructed on the pack. When cooked (it should be just tender, or *al dente*), drain. Add the tuna and coriander to the tomato sauce to heat through, and check the seasoning. Stir the sauce gently into the pasta and serve with the cheese sprinkled over.

NOTES AND TIPS
✦ *Vegetarians could omit the tuna and have extra cheese.*
✦ *Use less chilli if you don't like things quite so hot – or use the large green chillies only, which tend to be mild. The small red ones are usually the hottest. And don't add the seeds to a chilli dish unless you want your mouth burned!*

OPPOSITE: Fruit-filled Pancakes (page 129) and Summer Fruit Kebabs (page 130)

Prawn and Noodle Stir-fry

SERVES 2

CALORIES PER PORTION: 613	PROTEIN: HIGH
TOTAL FAT PER PORTION: 19g	CARBOHYDRATE: ★★
SATURATED FAT PER PORTION: 4g	FIBRE: ★★

I THINK I could eat noodles every day, if there weren't so many other foods I adored, too! One of their main blessings is the way they will cook within 4 minutes or so – ideal for the chef who is short of time. Team them with prawns, also almost-instant food, for the speediest meal ever.

2 flat cakes medium egg thread noodles (about 200g/7oz total weight)	½ teaspoon dried chilli flakes
1 tablespoon sesame oil	225g (8oz) peeled cooked prawns
50g (2oz) sugar snap peas or mangetout	2 teaspoons light soy sauce
4 spring onions, trimmed and halved lengthways	1 generous tablespoon oyster sauce
½ teaspoon Chinese five-spice seasoning	1 tablespoon fish stock or water
½ teaspoon ground ginger	2 teaspoons sesame oil to garnish

Bring a pan of water to the boil, add the noodles and either cook for 3–4 minutes or leave to soak, according to pack instructions. Meanwhile, heat the oil in a wok or non-stick frying pan and stir-fry the sugar snaps or mangetout for 2 minutes. Add the spring onions and all the spices, and stir-fry again for 1 minute. Add the prawns and soy sauce and stir for another minute. Mix the oyster sauce with the stock or water. Drain the noodles and add them to the pan with the oyster sauce mix. Stir for 1 minute, then serve with the sesame oil drizzled over.

NOTES AND TIPS
✦ *You can vary this recipe by using plum sauce instead of oyster sauce. You get a sweeter result which is equally tasty.*

Ciabatta Pizza

<u>SERVES 2</u>

CALORIES PER PORTION: 338	PROTEIN: HIGH
TOTAL FAT PER PORTION: 13g	CARBOHYDRATE: ★★
SATURATED FAT PER PORTION: 3.5g	FIBRE: ★★

A CROSS between a pizza and a bruschetta, this ciabatta pizza is excellent cold-weather comfort food.

2 medium tomatoes (about 150g/5½oz total weight)	2 teaspoons tomato purée
	3 slices prosciutto (Parma ham) (about 35g/1½oz)
1 yellow pepper, de-seeded and sliced	4 pitted black olives, chopped
1 tablespoon olive oil	2 tablespoons grated half-fat Mozzarella cheese
½ ciabatta loaf (see note)	fresh herbs, e.g. thyme, oregano, basil, to garnish
1 clove garlic	

Preheat the grill. Cut one of the tomatoes into quarters. Put the yellow pepper and tomato quarters on a baking tray or on foil on the grill rack and drizzle half the olive oil over. Put under the grill. Meanwhile, toast the ciabatta on both sides, then rub the cut side with the garlic and spread the tomato purée and remaining olive oil on top. Slice the remaining tomato and arrange the slices over the tomato purée. When the pepper is beginning to char, turn the slices and the tomato and grill on the other side for a few minutes. When nice and soft and speckled black all over, arrange the pepper slices and the cooked tomato on the bread and top with the ham, olives, cheese and herbs. Pop the bread under the grill – this time further away from the heat – until the top is bubbling. Serve immediately.

NOTES AND TIPS

✦ *You only need half a ciabatta loaf for this recipe. Cut the loaf in half through its length so that you have two flat, oblong halves. Freeze one half for another time.*

✦ *You can use ordinary extra-lean ham instead of the prosciutto if you like.*

✦ *You can bake the pizza for 15 minutes or so at 200°C/400°F/Gas Mark 6 rather than grilling it.*

Tuna and Tomato Pitta Pizza

SERVES 2

CALORIES PER PORTION: 418	PROTEIN: HIGH
TOTAL FAT PER PORTION: 6.5 g	CARBOHYDRATE: ★★★
SATURATED FAT PER PORTION: 2.5 g	FIBRE: ★★

A PITTA bread makes a quick and easy base for all your favourite pizza flavours; it's a little less calorific than an ordinary ready-made pizza base.

2 medium tomatoes	4 pitted black olives
½ small jar ready-made pizza topping (about	2 spring onions, finely chopped
75 g/3 oz)	2 teaspoons finely chopped fresh parsley
2 large pitta breads	3 tablespoons grated half-fat Mozzarella cheese
100 g (3½ oz) can tuna in brine, drained and flaked	

Preheat the grill. Slice the tomatoes thickly and place on foil on the grill rack or on a baking tray, and grill for 5 minutes or until soft. Meanwhile, spread the pizza topping on the pittas. Arrange the softened sliced tomatoes on top, and then the tuna, olives, spring onions and parsley. Top with the cheese and put back under the grill until bubbling and golden.

NOTES AND TIPS

✦ *You could use grated half-fat Edam or Cheddar-style cheese if you can't get Mozzarella.*

French Bread Pepperoni Pizza

SERVES 2

CALORIES PER PORTION: 375	PROTEIN: HIGH
TOTAL FAT PER PORTION: 11g	CARBOHYDRATE: ★★★
SATURATED FAT PER PORTION: 4g	FIBRE: ★★

BECAUSE French bread is so crusty it seems as if you are eating more than you actually are – unlike the great British sliced white loaf which leaves you wondering if you ate anything at all. This pizza topping is hot and spicy – ideal for winter.

150g (5½oz) French bread	1 ripe tomato, thinly sliced
½ small jar ready-made pizza topping (about 75g/3oz)	½ teaspoon dried chilli flakes *or* 1 teaspoon finely chopped fresh red chilli
3 tablespoons grated half-fat Mozzarella cheese	1 small red onion, very finely chopped
4 mushrooms, sliced	½ small green pepper, de-seeded and finely chopped
12 slices pepperoni (see note)	

Preheat the oven to 200°C/400°F/Gas Mark 6. Halve the French bread lengthways, and then slice a little of the crust off the rounded sides so that the pieces will sit on a plate without rocking. Top the cut sides of the bread with the pizza topping, and then sprinkle a quarter of the cheese on each one. Add the mushrooms, pepperoni and tomato, and scatter on the chilli flakes, red onion and green pepper. Finish with the remaining cheese. Bake in the oven for 15 minutes or until the cheese is bubbling and golden and the pepperoni browned.

NOTES AND TIPS
✦ *You can buy packs of mini pepperoni slices from the delicatessen section of your supermarket. Take out what you need for this recipe and freeze the rest.*

CHAPTER TEN

SALADS

All slimmers crave chocolate and loathe salads.

Yes, that's a slight exaggeration – but only slight! Most people I know who need to lose weight dread the thought of giving up such things as chocolate and butter, and have nightmares about endless dreary salad days stretching ahead of them. In fact, no slimmer need give up chocolate completely. And no slimmer need fear the dreaded salad – on two counts. First, you don't actually *have* to eat salad in order to lose weight if you don't want to – hot vegetables will do just as well as, or even better than, a plate of lettuce and tomato. And, second, salad can be as exciting, tasty, interesting and filling as you want it to be.

But it has to be said that not all salads are saintly. Indeed, certain classic salads – such as Waldorf and Caesar – are just about as high in calories as a box of chocolates, with as much fat in them as a plate of steak and chips. It's the salad dressings that are the culprits here. So beware of dolloping mayonnaise or French dressing with abandon on your own salads in order to make the cucumber and the lettuce leaves less boring. And forget about buying too many of those pre-packed salads, such as coleslaws, potato salads, rice salads, and so on, from the supermarket – unless specifically labelled 'low in fat', they will be far higher in calories than you could imagine, again because of their dressings. Another type of salad to avoid most of the time are those pretty little jars of Mediterranean-type mixes, often on the supermarket shelves near the pasta sauces. They contain such things as mixed mushrooms, mixed peppers, or various vegetables, and almost all come in pure oil. They may not be unhealthy (especially if the oil is olive oil) but they are extremely calorific.

So what sort of salad *should* a slimmer eat that is both tasty and not too high in calories? Well, the salads in this chapter – all complete meals in themselves – are good examples. Your salad should have plenty of carbohydrate in it, such as rice, pasta, couscous or potatoes (or be served with bread); it should contain plenty of vegetables and sometimes fruit, both of which should be fresh, to help bulk the salad out and provide vitamins and minerals, colour and crunch; it should contain some protein – meat, poultry, fish, low-fat dairy, eggs, pulses or tofu; it should be flavoured with appropriate herbs and/or spices and seasonings (either added separately or as part of the dressing); and, lastly, it should be tossed in a dressing that is tasty and appropriate but not high in fat or calories. And that last is often the hardest part of decent, low-calorie salad making.

Some of my favourite dressings that fit the bill are based on low-fat Bio yogurt, others on low-fat fromage frais or a dressing made by Kraft that is 70 per cent fat free but tastes like mayonnaise. Sometimes I use a little olive or other oil, though in nowhere near such large quantities as in a traditional vinaigrette, with rare exceptions. To this I usually add a piquancy with such things as lemon juice, lime juice, wine vinegar, balsamic vinegar (which can be used on its own as it is rich and sweet), soy sauce or mustard. The dressing may need a pinch of sugar, or a little honey or artificial sweetener and lastly you can add whatever herbs or spices you fancy. Taste as you go along and don't be afraid to experiment. Don't be stingy with your dressing – many salads, particularly those containing pasta, potatoes or rice, need plenty of 'lubrication'.

Salads don't have to be cold, either, nor made from only raw ingredients. Cooked vegetables marry well with raw salad items. Experiment! Experiment! And never say salads are boring again!

Side salads are a slightly different thing – you should omit the protein and carbohydrate and just dish up a delectable side plate of mixed leaves, or just one or two types of vegetables, e.g. onion and tomato.

New York Pastrami Salad

CALORIES PER PORTION: 330	PROTEIN: HIGH
TOTAL FAT PER PORTION: 7 g	CARBOHYDRATE: ★★★
SATURATED FAT PER PORTION: 1.5 g	FIBRE: ★★

PEOPLE rarely think to include fruit in their salads, apart from the odd bits of apple in a Waldorf or maybe some chopped diced fruit in a rice salad. But 'sweet and savoury' salads are delicious – try experimenting. This salad of pastrami and banana is a great start.

100 g (3½ oz) firm salad leaves, e.g. Cos, Little Gem, radicchio	a few poppy or sesame seeds to garnish
	2 bagels or rolls and a little low-fat spread to serve
1 carrot, grated	**Dressing**
1 gherkin, chopped	1 tablespoon natural low-fat Bio yogurt
6 cherry tomatoes, halved	1 tablespoon reduced-calorie ('light') mayonnaise
1 banana	1 tablespoon 0% fat fromage frais
50 g (2 oz) wafer-thin pastrami (see note)	2 teaspoons lemon juice

Mix together all the dressing ingredients. Mix the salad leaves in a serving bowl with the carrot, gherkin and cherry tomatoes. Peel the banana and slice thinly, and cut the pastrami into strips. Add both to the bowl. Spoon the dressing over and mix lightly. Garnish with the seeds. Serve with the bagels or rolls spread with low-fat spread.

NOTES AND TIPS
✦ *Find pastrami at the delicatessen counter of your local supermarket.*
✦ *Don't slice the banana until you are ready to combine the salad or it will go brown (unless you toss it in lemon juice).*

Salmon Salad with Pesto

SERVES 2

CALORIES PER PORTION: 430	PROTEIN: HIGH
TOTAL FAT PER PORTION: 28.5 g	CARBOHYDRATE: ★
SATURATED FAT PER PORTION: 5.5 g	FIBRE: ★★

FOR some reason, salmon and pesto go incredibly well together – they are both gutsy, strong-flavoured foods and you might think the combination would be too much, but it isn't. Pesto is high in oil and calories but in this recipe you don't need to use a lot.

100 g (3½ oz) pasta (farfalle or fusilli would be fine)	50 g (2 oz) frozen petits pois
	2 tablespoons ready-made fresh pesto (see note)
200 g (7 oz) salmon fillet	2 tablespoons Kraft 70% fat free mayonnaise
100 g (3½ oz) asparagus tips or canned artichoke hearts, drained	salt and freshly ground black pepper
	fresh herbs, e.g. basil, dill or tarragon, to garnish

Put a pan of salted water on to boil, and, when boiling, add the pasta. Boil, uncovered, for 12 minutes or as instructed on the pack. Drain, rinse with cold water and set aside. While the pasta is boiling, microwave or poach the salmon fillet until just cooked – about 3 minutes on medium in the microwave and the same if poaching. Drain and flake, removing any dark skin.

Bring a small saucepan of lightly salted water to the boil and blanch the asparagus tips, if using, for 2–3 minutes, adding the peas for the last 1½ minutes. Drain, rinse under cold running water, drain again thoroughly and set aside. If using artichoke hearts, pat them dry on absorbent kitchen paper and halve. In a small bowl, mix together the pesto, mayonnaise and seasoning. Combine all the ingredients in a serving bowl and sprinkle on the fresh herbs. Serve the salad at room temperature.

NOTES AND TIPS

◆ *Most supermarkets now stock fresh pesto in their chilled sauces cabinet. If you can't find the chilled sort, use a jar and, if possible, brighten it up a bit with some chopped fresh basil tossed into the dressing.*

◆ *If you would like a more liquid sauce, add some oil-free French dressing to the pesto/mayonnaise mix.*

Tabbouleh with Egg

<u>SERVES 2</u>

CALORIES PER PORTION: 374	PROTEIN: MEDIUM
TOTAL FAT PER PORTION: 24.5 g	CARBOHYDRATE: ★
SATURATED FAT PER PORTION: 4.5 g	FIBRE: ★

I LOVE tabbouleh – a bulghar wheat salad – with its clean, fresh flavour of mint and coolness of cucumber. This is a variation which adds protein to the dish – and it's a combination that works very well. It is quite high in total fat but very low in saturated fat.

60 g (2½ oz) bulghar wheat	I rounded tablespoon chopped fresh parsley
400 ml (¾ pint) hot vegetable stock	4 spring onions, chopped
2 medium eggs	3 tablespoons olive oil
lettuce leaves	I tablespoon lemon juice
I tasty ripe tomato, de-seeded and chopped	salt and freshly ground black pepper
4 cm (1½ inch) piece cucumber, chopped	fresh mint or parsley sprigs to garnish
I rounded tablespoon chopped fresh mint	

Put the bulghar wheat in a bowl and pour the hot stock over. Leave for 20 minutes during which time the wheat will absorb the stock and swell. Meanwhile, boil the eggs for 8 minutes, drain and rinse under cold, running water, then shell and quarter.

Line two serving bowls with the lettuce. In another bowl, mix together the tomato, cucumber, mint, parsley, spring onions, oil, lemon juice and seasoning. When the bulghar wheat is soaked, drain off any surplus stock and add the bulghar to the salad ingredients in the bowl, stirring well. Transfer to the serving bowls and serve garnished with the egg quarters and some fresh mint or parsley sprigs.

NOTES AND TIPS
✦ *For a side salad, you can omit the egg and serve the tabbouleh with grilled meats, such as lamb kebabs, or fish, such as grilled sardines.*

Hot Bacon, Mushroom and Avocado Salad

SERVES 2

CALORIES PER PORTION: 273	PROTEIN: HIGH
TOTAL FAT PER PORTION: 23.5 g	CARBOHYDRATE: ★
SATURATED FAT PER PORTION: 4.5 g	FIBRE: ★★

HERE are three of my favourite ingredients together in a delicious warm salad that is also a good starter if you serve half portions. Again, the total fat content is quite high but the saturated fat content is very low.

Fry Light cooking spray (see page 4)	50 g (2 oz) mixed firm salad leaves, e.g. Little Gem, Cos
3 rashers extra-lean back bacon, cut into strips	
1½ tablespoons olive oil	50 g (2 oz) oyster mushrooms, torn in half
150 g (5½ oz) mixed firm mushrooms, e.g. chestnut, button, halved if large	2 teaspoons red wine vinegar
	salt and freshly ground black pepper
1 clove garlic, crushed	5 cherry tomatoes, halved
1 small ripe avocado	2 tablespoons ready-made garlic croûtons

Heat a non-stick frying pan sprayed with Fry Light. Add the bacon while the pan is heating, and gradually increase the heat until the bacon cooks in its own fat. Don't stir until the underside is cooked or it might stick. When the bacon is golden, add half the oil, the firm mushrooms and the garlic, and fry for 3 minutes, stirring from time to time. Meanwhile, halve, stone, peel and slice the avocado, and arrange the salad leaves in a serving bowl. Add the rest of the oil, the oyster mushrooms, vinegar and seasoning to the frying pan, stir for 30 seconds, and toss the mushroom mixture into the serving bowl. Stir in the avocado and cherry tomatoes, and serve garnished with the croûtons.

NOTES AND TIPS

◆ *You can make your own croûtons if you like, by brushing bread with olive oil, cutting into squares and baking in the oven at 180°C/350°F/Gas Mark 4 for 15 minutes or until golden and crisp.*

◆ *Serve with some crusty bread to bring the total fat content down. Add 180 calories for a 50 g (2 oz) slice of French bread.*

Thai Prawn Salad

SERVES 2

CALORIES PER PORTION: 360	PROTEIN: HIGH
TOTAL FAT PER PORTION: 8.5 g	CARBOHYDRATE: ★★
SATURATED FAT PER PORTION: 1.5 g	FIBRE: ★

A HOT and spicy salad with a cooling rice and cucumber base. You will need some cold cooked rice – Thai or basmati.

225 g (8 oz) large prawns (tiger prawns would be ideal)	1 teaspoon caster sugar
1 clove garlic, chopped	225 g (8 oz) cold cooked Thai fragrant or basmati rice
½ teaspoon dried lemon grass	3 cm (1¼ inch) piece cucumber, chopped
1 small red chilli, de-seeded and finely chopped	1 tomato, de-seeded and chopped
½ teaspoon ground cumin	2 teaspoons chopped fresh coriander
1 tablespoon sesame oil	4 spring onions, trimmed, halved lengthways and cut into 2 cm (¾ inch) pieces
1 tablespoon light soy sauce	50 g (2 oz) beansprouts
2 teaspoons lime juice	

In a bowl, combine the prawns with the next eight ingredients. (If you now have time to leave this to stand for 30 minutes or so, so much the better. If not, proceed.) Mix together the rice, cucumber, tomato and coriander, and arrange in serving bowls. Heat a non-stick frying pan and add the prawns with their marinade, the onions and beansprouts, and stir for 2 minutes to heat through. Serve on the rice salad.

NOTES AND TIPS
✦ *You could use mixed ready-prepared seafood for this recipe, if you like. See page 71.*

Parma Salad

<u>SERVES 2</u>

CALORIES PER PORTION: 400	PROTEIN: HIGH
TOTAL FAT PER PORTION: 22.5 g	CARBOHYDRATE: ★
SATURATED FAT PER PORTION: 6 g	FIBRE: ★★

THIS salad combines several flavours from northern Italy – prosciutto (Parma ham), balsamic vinegar, Mozzarella cheese, plum tomatoes and dark salad leaves.

2 medium eggs	4 pitted black olives, halved
4 slices prosciutto (Parma ham) – about 30 g/1 oz	1½ tablespoons olive oil
50 g (2 oz) half-fat Mozzarella cheese (see note)	2 teaspoons balsamic vinegar
75 g (3 oz) dark salad leaves, e.g. spinach, watercress, lamb's lettuce, lollo rosso	pinch of mustard powder
	salt and freshly ground black pepper
2 plum tomatoes, roughly chopped	2 slices rustic Italian bread or similar to serve
1 small red onion, very thinly sliced	

Boil the eggs for 8 minutes, then drain, rinse under cold running water, shell and halve. Meanwhile, heat a non-stick frying pan containing the prosciutto, gradually increasing the heat, until the ham is crisp. Cut the cheese into thin slices. In a serving bowl, toss together the salad leaves, eggs, ham, cheese, tomatoes, onion and olives. Mix together the olive oil, vinegar, mustard and seasoning, and pour over the salad. Toss again. Serve with the bread.

NOTES AND TIPS

✦ *You can buy whole wrapped half-fat Mozzarella cheeses in most supermarkets, packed in brine. Open the pack, drain the brine off, cut off the amount of cheese you want and store the remainder, wrapped in foil in the fridge where it will keep for a few days. Slices of Mozzarella are very nice grilled with slices of beef tomato and dressed with balsamic vinegar and basil leaves as a light lunch.*

Chicken and Lentil Salad

<u>SERVES 2</u>

CALORIES PER PORTION: 212	PROTEIN: HIGH
TOTAL FAT PER PORTION: 7.5 g	CARBOHYDRATE: ★
SATURATED FAT PER PORTION: 1 g	FIBRE: ★★

A WONDERFUL combination of lightly spiced warm chicken, lentils and sweet peppers; this salad would be nice as part of a party buffet.

1 generous tablespoon natural low-fat Bio yogurt	1 clove garlic, crushed
1 cm (½ inch) garlic purée (from a tube)	75 g (3 oz) mixed sweet peppers in oil (drained
½ teaspoon garam masala	weight) (see note)
2 teaspoons plum sauce	1 tablespoon oil from sweet pepper jar
salt and freshly ground black pepper	2 teaspoons red wine vinegar
1 large skinned chicken breast fillet	pinch of sugar
100 g (3½ oz) canned green or brown lentils	selection of salad leaves
(drained weight)	

Preheat the grill. Mix the yogurt with the next four ingredients, and use to coat the chicken. Grill the chicken under a medium heat for 15 minutes, turning once or twice, until cooked. Meanwhile, mix the lentils, garlic and peppers in a bowl. Combine the oil, vinegar and sugar.

Arrange the salad leaves in a serving bowl. When the chicken is ready, cut it into diagonal slices about 1 cm (½ inch) thick and arrange on the salad leaves. Spoon the lentil and pepper mixture over and around the chicken, and spoon the dressing over the top.

NOTES AND TIPS
+ *Mixed sweet peppers come in pretty jars in the supermarket. Alternatively, you could used canned piquillo peppers or canned mixed peppers, and use 1 tablespoon olive oil instead of the sweet pepper oil. (Peppers are usually canned in water or brine, not oil.)*
+ *Serve with some wholemeal or dark rye bread.*

Couscous, Chickpea and Lamb Salad

SERVES 2

CALORIES PER PORTION: 334	PROTEIN: HIGH
TOTAL FAT PER PORTION: 9.5 g	CARBOHYDRATE: ★★
SATURATED FAT PER PORTION: 2.5 g	FIBRE: ★★

IF you have any leftover, pink-tinged roast lamb, this is an ideal way to use it up.

50 g (2 oz) couscous	¼ teaspoon ground coriander
200 ml (7 fl oz) vegetable or chicken stock, boiling	2 teaspoons chopped fresh mint
150 g (5½ oz) lean lamb leg meat, underdone, sliced	salt and freshly ground black pepper
2 tablespoons natural low-fat Bio yogurt	75 g (3 oz) canned chickpeas (drained weight)
1 small red pepper, de-seeded and thinly sliced	1 large tomato, de-seeded and chopped
2 teaspoons lime juice	a few fresh mint leaves
½ teaspoon ground cumin	a few red lettuce leaves, shredded, to garnish

Preheat the grill. Put the couscous in a bowl and add the hot stock. Leave to soak. Coat the lamb slices in half the yogurt and flash under the grill for 2 minutes each side with the red pepper slices. Mix together the remaining yogurt, lime juice, cumin, coriander, mint and seasoning.

When the couscous is ready, fluff it up with a fork and put it in serving dishes. Add the chickpeas, tomato and yogurt sauce, and stir in lightly. Add the meat and top with the pepper slices and mint leaves. Garnish with a few shredded red lettuce leaves. Serve at room temperature.

NOTES AND TIPS

◆ *You could use raw lamb fillet in this recipe, in which case slice thinly, coat with yogurt and cook under the grill for 3 minutes each side.*

Potato Salad with Saffron and Eggs

<u>SERVES 2</u>

CALORIES PER PORTION: 326	PROTEIN: HIGH
TOTAL FAT PER PORTION: 14.5g	CARBOHYDRATE: ★★
SATURATED FAT PER PORTION: 5g	FIBRE: ★★

I ADORE potato salad and usually make it with a parsley- and mint-rich vinaigrette dressing, but this one is delicious, too, and goes particularly well with eggs.

350 g (13 oz) well-flavoured new potatoes, scraped if necessary	150 ml (5½ fl oz) half-fat Greek-style yogurt
1 sachet saffron stamens	1 tablespoon light mayonnaise
2 medium eggs	1 tablespoon half-fat single cream
4 canned artichoke hearts, drained	1 teaspoon French mustard
2 teaspoons chopped garlic chives (see note)	salt and freshly ground black pepper
	1 butterhead lettuce, divided into leaves

Boil the potatoes in lightly salted water until tender but not broken up. Drain and, if necessary, cut into 2 cm (¾ inch) chunks. While the potatoes are boiling, soak the saffron in a little boiling water and boil the eggs for 8 minutes. Drain the eggs, rinse under cold running water, shell and roughly chop. Dry the artichoke hearts on absorbent kitchen paper. Mix together the garlic chives, yogurt, mayonnaise, cream, mustard and seasoning in a bowl. Add enough saffron water to colour the dressing a pretty yellow.

Line a serving dish with the lettuce and, when the potatoes are ready and still slightly warm, toss them into the bowl. Add the artichoke hearts and most of the egg, and pour the dressing over. Sprinkle the remaining egg on top and serve.

NOTES AND TIPS

✦ *If you haven't got any artichoke hearts, you could use some peas or asparagus tips instead.*

✦ *Non-vegetarians could add some crisply cooked lean bacon to this salad.*

✦ *Garlic chives are slightly thicker than ordinary chives and have a distinct garlicky taste. If you can't get them or grow them, use ordinary chives and add a little crushed garlic to the dressing.*

Greek Pasta Salad

<u>SERVES 2</u>

CALORIES PER PORTION: 392	PROTEIN: MEDIUM
TOTAL FAT PER PORTION: 19.5 g	CARBOHYDRATE: ★★
SATURATED FAT PER PORTION: 7 g	FIBRE: ★★

EVERYONE loves Greek salad – for a change, try it with pasta.

100 g (3½ oz) penne (pasta tubes)	1 small green pepper, de-seeded and sliced
2 ripe tomatoes, roughly chopped	1½ tablespoons olive oil
8 pitted black olives, halved	2 teaspoons lemon juice
75 g (3 oz) Feta cheese, crumbled	2 teaspoons chopped fresh herbs, e.g. oregano,
4 spring onions, chopped *or* 1 small mild onion,	thyme, mint
sliced	salt and freshly ground black pepper

Put a pan of salted water on to boil and, when boiling, add the pasta. Boil, uncovered, for 12 minutes or as instructed on the pack. When the pasta is cooked (it should be just tender, or *al dente*), drain it. While the pasta is cooking, prepare all the other ingredients and make the dressing by combining the olive oil, lemon juice, herbs and seasoning. When the pasta is still slightly warm, toss it with the salad ingredients and the dressing, and serve.

NOTES AND TIPS
✦ *If you prefer a moister salad, add some oil-free French dressing to taste, or some balsamic vinegar.*

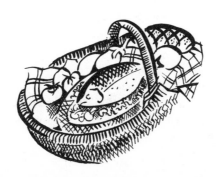

CHAPTER ELEVEN

DESSERTS

If you are slimming, there is no need to think that you won't be able to eat a wicked-tasting dessert again until the diet is over. Admittedly, it is hard to fit a large slice of chocolate gâteau or banoffee pie into a healthy reduced-calorie plan – but there are plenty of ways of getting similar *tastes* and *richness* into much lower-calorie, lower-fat desserts that *can* form part of your diet. As you will have seen from the diet plans in chapter 2 (pages 19–24), the desserts in this chapter can all be eaten within a low-calorie diet.

My main criterion for choosing suitable recipes for this chapter was that the desserts should all offer something positive to your day's nutrition, rather than simply being very low in calories. Most contain fresh fruit, which supplies vitamin C, fibre, and often many other vitamins and minerals too; many contain low-fat dairy products, which provide calcium – much needed, especially by women, in a slimming diet to help keep bones strong and dense.

Here are some more quick ideas for healthy desserts that aren't very high in calories:

★ Half-fat Greek yogurt layered in a glass with fresh berries and sprinkled with luxury muesli.
★ A fresh fruit salad on a one-colour theme (e.g. all green fruits, all red fruits, all orange fruits) with a fruit juice of a suitable colour (e.g. apple juice for a green salad) poured over and served with a spoonful of 8 per cent fat fromage frais.
★ A fresh dessert pear, quartered and cored, and topped with a little ground cinnamon, raspberry sorbet and a spoonful of 8 per cent fat fromage frais.
★ Two fresh figs, halved and served with a very thin slice of Brie.
★ A scoop of low-calorie ice cream served with fresh strawberries dusted with icing sugar and a sauce made by puréeing the contents of a can of apricots in natural juice.

Tiramisu

<u>SERVES 4</u>

CALORIES PER PORTION: 234
TOTAL FAT PER PORTION: 12g
SATURATED FAT PER PORTION: 8.5 g

PROTEIN: MEDIUM
CARBOHYDRATE: ★
FIBRE: ★

ALTHOUGH no longer the fashionable dessert it was, nevertheless I have yet
to meet anyone who doesn't like this rich, creamy taste sensation. Normally
absolutely stuffed full of calories, tiramisu is never going to be a very low-
calorie dessert – but I've reduced the fat as much as possible here to bring it
within the bounds of possibility as a fairly regular treat, and, to my mind, the
lighter texture is even nicer than the original. You can halve the quantities
to serve two, double them for eight, or whatever, as long as you use a
suitable-sized container. (If making it for two, I would use individual glasses.)

75 g (3 oz) Mascarpone cheese	50 ml (2 fl oz) coffee liqueur or brandy
200 g (7 oz) 8% fat fromage frais	75 ml (3 fl oz) strong coffee
75 g (3 oz) half-fat Greek yogurt	10 sponge fingers
25 g (1 oz) fructose (see note)	cocoa powder to decorate

In a bowl, beat together the cheeses and yogurt and add the fructose. In a
wide, shallow bowl, mix together the coffee liqueur or brandy and the
coffee, and dip the sponge fingers into the mixture one by one, then
remove. Layer the cheese mixture and fingers in a suitable glass bowl,
starting with a third of the cheese, then half the sponge fingers, then another
third of the cheese, then the rest of the fingers, and finally the last of the
cheese. Sift some cocoa powder over the top and chill for as long as you can
– up to 24 hours.

NOTES AND TIPS
✦ *If you want an even lighter tiramisu, whisk an egg white until it forms soft peaks
and fold it gently into the cheese mixture before assembling as above.*
✦ *Fructose is a fruit sugar that has the same calorie content as ordinary sugar (sucrose)
but is much sweeter so you can use less in your recipes. It is also better for you,
being absorbed into the bloodstream more slowly than sucrose.*

Poached Pears

SERVES 2

CALORIES PER PORTION: 188	PROTEIN: LOW
TOTAL FAT PER PORTION: TRACE	CARBOHYDRATE: ★★★
SATURATED FAT PER PORTION: TRACE	FIBRE: ★★

THIS quick and easy dessert never fails to please, and it is fat free and very low in calories, too.

2 large pears	40 g (1½ oz) fructose (see page 125)
1 tablespoon lemon juice	1 cinnamon stick
150 ml (5½ fl oz) red wine	

Peel the pears and cut each lengthways into eight. Remove the cores. Drop the pears into lemon juice as you do this to stop them browning. Heat the wine and fructose in a saucepan until the fructose has dissolved. Add the pears and cinnamon stick, cover and poach gently for 25 minutes or until tender, basting occasionally with the wine so that the pears take up a lovely ruby red colour. Remove the pears when cooked, turn up the heat and reduce the remaining liquid until you have a syrupy sauce. Remove the cinnamon stick, pour the sauce over the pears, and serve.

NOTES AND TIPS

✦ *You can use water instead of wine, or half water and half wine, or any fruit juice mixture.*

✦ *The pears are nice served with yogurt ice cream.*

Fruit Selection with Chocolate Dip

SERVES 4

CALORIES PER PORTION: 174
TOTAL FAT PER PORTION: 7.5 g
SATURATED FAT PER PORTION: 4.5 g

PROTEIN: LOW
CARBOHYDRATE: ★★★
FIBRE: ★

HERE'S a healthy way to eat chocolate, if there is such a thing! Lovely summer fresh fruits dipped into a melted chocolate sauce – fabulous!

150 g (5½ oz) strawberries	100 g (3½ oz) chocolate of choice, white, dark or
2 peaches	milk
150 g (5½ oz) fresh pineapple chunks	

Hull the strawberries, stone and slice the peaches, and arrange all the fruit on four serving plates. Put the chocolate in a heatproof bowl over a pan of simmering water (making sure the bowl doesn't touch the water) and melt the chocolate. Serve the melted chocolate as a dipping sauce for the fruit.

NOTES AND TIPS
✦ *Vary the fruit according to what is available.*

Grilled Bananas

SERVES 2

CALORIES PER PORTION: 168
TOTAL FAT PER PORTION: 3.5 g
SATURATED FAT PER PORTION: 2 g

PROTEIN: LOW
CARBOHYDRATE: ★★★
FIBRE: ★

A QUICK hot dessert, ideal for winter.

2 large bananas	pinch of ground mixed spice or cinnamon
25 ml (1 fl oz) orange juice	2 teaspoons brown sugar
15 g (½ oz) half-fat Anchor	

Preheat the grill. Peel the bananas, cut them in half lengthways and toss in the orange juice in a shallow heatproof dish. Mix together the 'butter', spice and sugar in a small bowl and dot the bananas with this mixture. Grill the bananas quite near the heat for 6–7 minutes, turning once, or until they are golden. Serve immediately.

NOTES AND TIPS
✦ *The bananas should be slightly under-ripe if possible and definitely not over-ripe.*
✦ *For a treat, add a little orange-flavoured liqueur to the orange juice.*

Fruit-filled Pancakes

<u>SERVES 4</u>

CALORIES PER PORTION: 166	PROTEIN: LOW
TOTAL FAT PER PORTION: 3.5 g	CARBOHYDRATE: ★★★
SATURATED FAT PER PORTION: 1 g	FIBRE: ★★

A NICE autumn pudding, this is quicker to make than you'd think. It's hardly worth making pancake batter just for two people, so this serves four. But if there are only two of you, the remaining batter, or the made-up pancakes, can be frozen.

75 g (3 oz) plain flour	450 g (1 lb) mixed fresh fruit of choice, e.g. dessert
1 medium egg	plums, dessert pears, apples, grapes, berries,
75 ml (3 fl oz) skimmed milk	peaches
25 ml (1 fl oz) water	about 2 teaspoons icing sugar
salt	4 tablespoons half-fat Greek yogurt or 8% fat
Fry Light cooking spray (see page 4)	fromage frais to serve

Put the flour in a bowl and beat in the egg, the milk mixed with the water, and a pinch of salt. When the mix is smooth, heat an omelette pan sprayed with Fry Light. While the pan is heating, prepare the fruit if necessary, e.g. stone and chop plums or peaches, core and chop apples. All the fruit should be in small bite-sized pieces. Drizzle a little icing sugar over the fruit.

Spoon a little of the pancake mixture into the pan, swirl around and cook for 1 minute until the underside is flecked golden. Turn the pancake with a spatula and cook the other side, then remove to a serving dish and keep warm. Make seven more pancakes this way, and then fill each one with a little of the fruit mixture. Sift some icing sugar over and serve with the yogurt or fromage frais.

NOTES AND TIPS

◆ *If the prepared fruit is to stand around for a while, it is wise to toss it in lemon juice otherwise some fruits, such as apples, pears and bananas, will discolour.*

Summer Fruit Kebabs

CALORIES PER PORTION: 188

TOTAL FAT PER PORTION: 0.5 g

SATURATED FAT PER PORTION: TRACE

PROTEIN: LOW

CARBOHYDRATE: ★★★

FIBRE: ★★

HERE'S a pretty idea that makes a change from fruit salad, which can get marginally boring if you're on a diet.

I banana	2 teaspoons orange-flavoured liqueur
I nectarine	I small can apricots in natural juice
6 medium-large strawberries, hulled	2 teaspoons fructose (see page 125)
2 teaspoons runny honey	

Preheat the grill. Peel the banana and cut it into bite-sized cubes. Stone the nectarine and cut it into segments, then halve each segment. Thread all the fruits evenly on to kebab skewers. Blend the honey and liqueur in a small bowl and brush over the fruits. Put the kebabs under the grill and heat, basting from time to time with the extra liqueur mix. Meanwhile, drain the apricots, reserving the juice. Put the apricots in a blender with the fructose and blend to a purée. Thin the purée with as much apricot juice as you need to make a smooth pouring sauce.

When the kebabs are turning golden, serve them with any remaining basting sauce and the apricot sauce spooned over them.

NOTES AND TIPS

✦ *You could use oranges, pears and pineapple for a winter kebab.*

Creamed Plums

SERVES 2

CALORIES PER PORTION: 177	PROTEIN: LOW
TOTAL FAT PER PORTION: 3 g	CARBOHYDRATE: ★★★
SATURATED FAT PER PORTION: 2 g	FIBRE: ★

THIS simply gorgeous dessert proves that you don't have to spend ages in the kitchen to provide something delectable.

300 g (11 oz) can red plums, drained	50 ml (2 fl oz) low-fat custard
50 ml (2 fl oz) fromage frais	1 tablespoon caster sugar
50 ml (2 fl oz) half-fat Greek yogurt	

Preheat the grill. Stone the plums, if necessary, and place in a shallow heatproof dish of the right size to just contain them in one layer. Beat together the fromage frais, yogurt and custard, and pour over the plums. Sprinkle over half the sugar. Cook under the grill, a medium distance from the heat, until the creamed mixture bubbles and forms a skin, then sprinkle on the remaining sugar and put back under the grill to turn slightly golden. Serve straight away.

NOTES AND TIPS
✦ *You could use fresh plums in this dish but you would have to halve and stone them, then poach them lightly in water for about 15 minutes or until tender before proceeding as above.*

Peach Melba

CALORIES PER PORTION: 167	PROTEIN: LOW
TOTAL FAT PER PORTION: 8 g	CARBOHYDRATE: ★★
SATURATED FAT PER PORTION: 1 g	FIBRE: ★

THIS is a splendid summer dessert to put together in a minute or two.

I teaspoon arrowroot	75 g (3 oz) raspberries
50 ml (2 fl oz) orange juice	2 tablespoons half-fat Greek yogurt
I ripe peach	2 teaspoons chopped mixed nuts
2 scoops reduced-calorie raspberry ripple ice cream	

Blend the arrowroot with a little of the orange juice. Heat the remaining orange juice in a small saucepan and add the arrowroot, stirring until the juice thickens to a sauce. Remove from the heat and reserve. Stone and slice the peach and arrange in two serving dishes. Put the ice cream scoops on top, then half the raspberries, then pour over the orange sauce. Spoon on the yogurt, top with the remaining raspberries and sprinkle on the nuts. Serve at once.

Rhubarb Fool

CALORIES PER PORTION: 127	PROTEIN: MEDIUM
TOTAL FAT PER PORTION: 4.5 g	CARBOHYDRATE: ★★
SATURATED FAT PER PORTION: 2.5 g	FIBRE: ★

RHUBARB is one of my favourite fruits and I don't know why it isn't more popular. It's around in quantity in the spring when there is little else locally grown available, and contains hardly any calories at all.

225 g (8 oz) tender young rhubarb stalks	pinch of ground mixed spice
I tablespoon orange juice	100 ml (3½ fl oz) half-fat Greek yogurt
25 g (I oz) fructose (see page 125)	50 ml (2 fl oz) 8% fat fromage frais

Chop the rhubarb and put it in a saucepan with the orange juice. Cover and cook on a medium heat for 10 minutes or until the rhubarb is tender. Allow to cool a little, then add the fructose and spice. Meanwhile, beat together the yogurt and fromage frais, then combine the rhubarb with the yogurt mixture and divide between two glasses. Chill if you have time before serving.

NOTES AND TIPS
✦ *Gooseberries make a nice fool for later in the year.*

Pineapple Flambé

SERVES 2

CALORIES PER PORTION: 137	PROTEIN: LOW
TOTAL FAT PER PORTION: 3.5 g	CARBOHYDRATE: ★★★
SATURATED FAT PER PORTION: 2 g	FIBRE: ★

A JUICY fresh pineapple is a treat in itself, but for a little luxury, try this.

300 g (II oz) fresh pineapple (prepared weight)	I tablespoon rum
15 g (½ oz) half-fat Anchor	pinch of ground cinnamon
I tablespoon caster sugar	

If you need to prepare the pineapple, peel it and cut into 2 cm (³⁄₄ inch) slices. Using a sharp knife, remove the 'eyes' from around the edge of each slice, and then cut the slices into chunks. Melt the 'butter' in a non-stick frying pan. Meanwhile, toss the pineapple in the sugar. Add the pineapple chunks to the pan and fry for 1–2 minutes on each side. Add the rum and carefully ignite with a match or taper. When the flames have died down, cook the pineapple a little longer, turning occasionally. Serve with the cinnamon sprinkled over.

NOTES AND TIPS
✦ *This goes well with vanilla ice cream.*

INDEX